D1562380

DATE DUE

Unless Recalled Earlier

DEMCO, INC. 38-2931

Eight Ways to Run the Country

Eight Ways to Run the Country

A New and Revealing Look at Left and Right

Brian Patrick Mitchell

Westport, Connecticut
London

Library of Congress Cataloging-in-Publication Data

Mitchell, Brian Patrick.
  Eight ways to run the country : a new and revealing look at left and right / Brian
Patrick Mitchell.
       p.   cm.
  Includes bibliographical references and index.
  ISBN 0–275–99358–2 (alk. paper)
  1. Political culture—United States.   2. United States—Politics and government—1989–
3. Right and left (Political science).   I. Title.
JK1726.M58   2007
320.50973–dc22   2006028561

British Library Cataloguing in Publication Data is available.

Library of Congress Catalog Card Number: 2006028561
ISBN: 0–275–99358–2

First published in 2007

Praeger Publishers, 88 Post Road West, Westport, CT 06881
An imprint of Greenwood Publishing Group, Inc.
www.praeger.com

Printed in the United States of America

The paper used in this book complies with the
Permanent Paper Standard issued by the National
Information Standards Organization (Z39.48–1984).

10 9 8 7 6 5 4 3 2 1

Copyright Acknowledgment

The author and the publisher gratefully acknowledge permission to excerpt material from
the following source:

"Paradise" by John Prine. Words and Music by John Prine. Copyright © 1970 (Renewed)
Walden Music, Inc. All Rights Reserved. Used by Permission of Alfred Publishing Co., Inc.

To my mother,
JEAN YOUNG MITCHELL,
And to my late father,
JOHN TILLMAN MITCHELL JR.
1926–1990
May God grant her many years
and keep him in eternal memory.

Contents

Preface

This book began as a reflection on the collapse of Soviet communism and the presidential election of 1992. The reflection inspired a theory of ideological difference based on a distinction of the social and the political. Americans, it seemed to me then, were either for or against the social institutions of family, church, and corporation, and they were either for or against the political institutions of government.

The theory was set forth in an essay accepted for publication by the journal *Theologies & Moral Concerns* in 1993 but not published until 1995. In the long wait for the essay to be published, my attention was drawn elsewhere. I did not begin work on a book based on the theory until the spring of 2001. The theory seemed then as valid and useful as ever, but in thinking things through I was forced to refine my understanding of the distinction at the heart of the theory. It still seemed that people could be for or against government and for or against the social institutions of family, church, and corporation, but just what was it about each that some people disliked?

The question forced me to reduce the theory's fundamental distinction to the simplest concepts possible. Instead of the social and the political, I recast the theory in terms of rank and force. To varying degrees, people are either for or against the concept of rank, and they are either for or against the use of force. This distinction has a historical basis in actual institutions and events that have goaded our thinking in different directions, producing the furious diversity characteristic of modern Western political thought. Its elemental concepts still peak up at us from some of the words we use, but for too long they have been obscured by arguments over power and authority, hierarchy and equality, monarchy and democracy, autocracy and autonomy, authenticity and oppression. As a result, some people recognize no distinction between rank and force, believing that all hierarchies are inherently coercive, but others do recognize the distinction, and the difference between those who do and those who don't is part of the broader scheme of differences that this book will explain.

The book offers a conceptual framework to help readers recognize the divergent perspectives in current contention, providing readers with a few new terms and a new political Compass as an aid to understanding. The Compass correctly pegs the ideological poles. It doesn't do away with Left and Right; instead, it defines Left and Right in better terms and adds a whole new dimension to explain what Left and Right can't. The book untangles the historical threads of our political heritage, to identify four main traditions in American political thinking stretching back several centuries. Two of these traditions lead us leftward, but only one is represented today by the Democratic Party. Over time, the four traditions have given rise to eight distinct and divergent political perspectives evident today. Each of these appears in varying degrees of definition—vague and populist toward the center of the compass, mixed and moderate along the Compass's circumference, sharply ideological further out. The book devotes a chapter to each of the eight perspectives, naming a half-dozen or so notable persons as examples and using their own words to paint each portrait. A final chapter assesses the current situation, in light of past shifts of power among the eight perspectives, and looks ahead to future possibilities.

During the writing of the essay and the book, ideological diversity was a hot topic. In both 1992 and 2000, the major parties struggled to define themselves in the post-Reagan, post-Cold War world. Third parties played a decisive role as spoilers in both presidential elections. The opposition of Left and Right appeared increasingly inadequate to explain anything other than the contest between Republicans and Democrats, while the World Wide Web was introducing more and more Americans to more and more alternatives.

The terrorist attacks of September 11, 2001, and the invasion of Iraq in 2003 for a while overwhelmed the growing interest in political alternatives, however. On one hand, the stark contrast between Islam and the West dwarfed Western differences. On the other hand, the passionate polarization of American politics overrode other concerns. As during the Cold War, the world's choices seemed simply black and white, while the nation's choices seemed simply red and blue.

But September 11 did not in fact bring enough moral clarity to unite the country ideologically, and continuing troubles in Iraq now threaten to deal a reversal to Republican fortunes, in the wake of which we can only expect more soul-searching and dissent. This book will educate the reader on what to expect. Those who seek only to win elections may read other books. Those who seek first to understand must read this one.

For several years after September 11, it seemed impossible to publish a book about politics that did not plainly scream at one side or the other. I owe my success with this book to many friends who believed in it. Alex Hoyt, my agent, never gave up on the book. Hilary Claggett, my editor at Praeger, was smart enough to see what Hoyt saw. Saloni Jain of Techbooks managed the copyediting with kind consideration of the author's preferences, from as far away as Delhi, India. Professors Jon Lauck, Chris Sciabarra, and Paul Gottfried reviewed the book, providing helpful criticism and guidance. James Jatras, Michael Lofgren, Aaron Steelman, David and Alida Kass, and Professor Claes Ryn read early drafts of the book and provided both comments and encouragement. John Sanders gave me valuable advice on the publishing industry. Kelly Kehrer provided prayers and exhortations at crucial moments. And finally, my wife Cindy endured two years of research and writing and then four years of waiting to see the book in print. Her patience is priceless.

Alexandria, Virginia
August 6, 2006

Chapter 1

Schizocracy in America

Let us at all times remember that all American citizens are brothers of a common country, and should dwell together in the bonds of fraternal feeling.

Abraham Lincoln, 1860

The September 11 terrorist attacks on the World Trade Center and the Pentagon united the nation as nothing since Pearl Harbor. Who was not stunned by the sight of jet airliners slamming into New York's twin towers, or the sight of both buildings suddenly crumbling to the ground? Americans flooded New York with extra help. They gave generously to relief organizations. Long-planned public events were canceled without a peep of protest. A contentious Congress laid aside all other earthly cares in a spirit of solemn bipartisanship. Utah Senator Orrin Hatch wrote a song entitled "Americans United," and President George W. Bush, in his address to Congress and the nation, plugged a Web site for volunteers, LibertyUnites.org.

But amazement at the attacks may have been the only thing that truly united all Americans, who, in fact, did not stand united in their views of the event or in their calls for action.

The very day of the attacks, Robert Kagan of the Carnegie Endowment for International Peace was already anticipating dissent—and writing to squelch it. In the next day's *Washington Post*, Kagan exhorted Americans to respond with "moral clarity and courage as our grandfathers did [after Pearl Harbor]. Not by asking what we have done to bring on the wrath of inhuman murderers. Not by figuring out ways to reason with, or try to appease those who have spilled our blood." Kagan called for Congress to declare war immediately on terrorists and "any nations that may have lent their support."

But many other Americans were less sanguine. Marxist historian Howard Zinn wailed that those who wanted war "have learned nothing, absolutely nothing" from the bloody twentieth century: "Isn't it clear by now that sending a message to terrorists through violence doesn't work, only leads to more terrorism? Haven't we learned anything from the Israeli-Palestinian conflict?"

Matthew Rothschild, editor of *The Progressive*, blamed terrorism on global poverty, bigotry, nationalism, and religious fanaticism, which he accused the United States of cultivating by training the Afghans to fight the Soviets, making war on Iraq, and backing Israel's repression of the Palestinians. The editors of *The Nation* recommended "returning to the treaties that the United States has recently been discarding" on global warming, nuclear, biological, and chemical weapons, and the International Criminal Court.

Harry Browne, past presidential candidate of the Libertarian Party, declared sanity the first casualty of the war. "Our foreign policy has been insane for decades," he wrote. "When will we learn that we can't allow our politicians to bully the world without someone bullying back eventually?"

The libertarian Cato Institute called for using "whatever military force necessary against the guilty parties" but advised against curtailing civil liberties for the sake of security. "There are those who would say that without security, freedom and liberty mean nothing," wrote Cato's Charles Peña. "I would argue that without the reality of freedom and liberty, the concepts of freedom and liberty mean nothing."

Thomas Fleming, president of the Rockford Institute, wrote that the attacks of September 11 "represent one battle in an ongoing war between two systems that seek to take over the earth: Islam and the post-Christian religion that leftists see as a planetary state and 'conservatives' see as 'benevolent global hegemony.' "

Patrick Buchanan, recalling that Ronald Reagan pulled U.S. troops out of Lebanon after terrorists blew up the Marine barracks in Beirut, recommended doing the same in the Middle East. "There is no vital American interest at risk in all these religious, territorial, and tribal wars from Algeria to Afghanistan," he wrote. "Let us pay back those who did this, then let us extricate ourselves. Either America finds an exit strategy from empire, or we lose our republic."

Evangelist Jerry Falwell blamed pagans, abortionists, feminists, gays, lesbians, the American Civil Liberties Union, the People for the American Way, and "all of them who have tried to secularize America. I point the finger in their face and say, 'You helped this happen,' " he said on television to fellow evangelist Pat Robertson. "God continues to lift the curtain and allow enemies of America to give us probably what we deserve." "Jerry, that's my feeling," Robertson replied.

Ken Connor, then president of the Family Research Council, responded saying, "This is not the time to further wound America's spirit, by casting blame on our fellow citizens. . . . Singling out groups whose conduct offends us is not likely to bring about the national repentance that our country needs." Both Falwell and Robertson later said their words were "harsh and ill-timed," "totally inappropriate," and "not fully understood." But neither said their words were inaccurate or untrue.

The American Prospect's Wendy Kaminer branded both men "our very own Taliban." "What's most striking about Falwell's rant is his assumption that God's presence in public life and government is always a public good," she wrote. "I'm not blaming religion for all or even most human barbarism"—but—"Whatever lessons we take from this dreadful attack, we should never forget that it was, after all, a faith-based initiative."

The Democratic Leadership Council rose to the defense of Muslims in America, pleading with Americans to "fight terrorism, not your neighbors." "We are not at war with Arabs, with Muslims, with immigrants, or with those who embrace unfamiliar culture," it declared. "We are at war with terrorists whose only real community is one formed by hatred of the values our country holds dear: freedom, tolerance, and diversity."

A DIVERSITY OF DIVISIONS

Diversity, indeed—factious, feuding diversity, a free-for-all of fear and fantasy raging right and left like the Gadarene swine.

The realities of power give us just two competitive choices on Election Day, but what each represents is a matter of constant contention. The United States has embarked on a great crusade to modernize and democratize less progressive regions of the world, and the party behind this "global democratic revolution" is the party of the Right—the supposedly conservative party. It has almost made sense of the media's red/blue switcheroo, which has Republicans and Democrats wearing each other's colors. The media would not have gotten away with it if Left and Right still stood for the same things.

But what did Left and Right stand for to begin with? That in itself has never been entirely clear. The opposition of Left and Right has been around since the French Revolution, but it was never much a part of American politics until the early twentieth century, when the conflict between communists and fascists seemed to catch most Americans in the middle.[1] Then the Left/Right spectrum looked to many like this:

Communist   Liberal   Conservative   Fascist

The second half of the twentieth century pitted communists against capitalists. This inspired a Cold War view of Left and Right, based on more or less government. The Left was *collectivist*; the Right, *individualist*. The spectrum looked like this:

Communist   Liberal   Conservative   Individualist

But neither spectrum pleased both the Left and the Right. Conservatives rejected the first, insisting that fascism was a form of socialism and therefore a leftist ideology. Liberals rejected the second, insisting that fascism was indeed right-wing and at least as great a threat as communism. They saw themselves as the sensible center of a spectrum that looked more like this:

Communist   Socialist   Liberal   Conservative   Fascist

But as the world grew more aware of Communist tyranny, it became harder and harder to maintain fascism and communism as polar opposites. Their real-world examples looked so much alike that some theorists have wondered whether the two might not converge at some point. The spectrum seemed to bend at the ends to form a horseshoe, left open at the top (or bottom) because the point of convergence of fascism and communism remained a mystery.

In 1964, German-born British psychologist Hans Eysenck put forth the first known bipolar scheme, adding an up-and-down opposition of authority and liberty to the familiar opposition of Left and Right. Personalities he described as "tough minded" (hostile, aggressive, domineering) tended toward authoritarianism, while "tender minded" personalities inclined toward liberality (see Figure 1.1). The theory fit the mid-century fashion of psychologizing political differences, pioneered in 1950 by Theodor Adorno and the other authors of *The Authoritarian Personality*. But whereas Adorno and his coauthors wrote to diagnose the Right as authoritarian, on account of its patriarchal social and religious traditions, Eysenck wrote to alert the liberal establishment to the "authoritarianism of the Left."

Eysenck's scheme made some sense, but it left unanswered difficult questions concerning the difference between Left and Right and the relation of personality to policy. Where on the scheme would we put tough-minded,

Figure 1.1
Hans Eysenck's Political Personalities

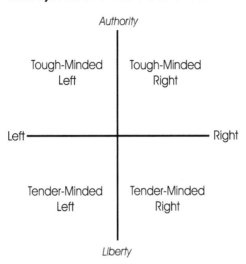

aggressive, capitalistic robber-barons who lobby hard for laissez-faire and low taxation? Why are women more likely than men to favor government assistance and regulation? What are liberty and authority anyway? Wouldn't everyone who aspires to lead tend toward the top of the tough/tender axis? Wouldn't all good citizens who faithfully follow their leaders tend toward the bottom? Wouldn't every society need some of both? How then should we run the country? Eysenck only warns us not to follow sociopaths, whatever their politics.

More recently, Adorno devotees in Britain tried to improve upon Eysenck's scheme with their own "Political Compass."[2] They made economics the difference between Left and Right and identified the vertical axis with a "social dimension"—meaning the coercive pressure of the community (see Figure 1.2). The problem here is the identification of Left and Right with economic freedom, opposing communism and European free-market "neoliberalism." This defies the historical origin of the Left/Right difference. Economics did not come to dominate the battle between Left and Right until the latter half of the nineteenth century, after both the Industrial Revolution and Karl Marx. Before that, European "liberals" took their seats on the left. They sometimes favored more economic freedom, but their driving passion from the start was not economics, but political and intellectual freedom. They were first and foremost free-thinkers and not always free-traders.

Figure 1.2
"The Political Compass"

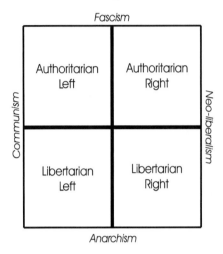

A six-page survey at www.politicalcompass.org lets you find yourself within the box. To its credit, the survey does tease out differences among "libertarians," but making the horizontal axis the scale of economic freedom shoves Milton Friedman and nearly all American libertarians to the far right—a clear indication that something's wrong. The scheme also leaves us with the perplexing possibility of communal fascism in the upper left and neoliberal fascism in the upper right, which can only make us wonder what fascism really is.

In 1970, libertarians came up with their own scheme based on a distinction of the social (or personal) and the economic. It seemed to David Nolan, founder of the Libertarian Party, that *conservatives* wanted to control personal behavior but not the economy, while *liberals* wanted to control the economy but not personal behavior. That left two other possibilities: *libertarians* who wanted to control nothing, and *authoritarians* who wanted to control everything. Nolan positioned his four players around a baseball diamond, with the first-base line as a scale of economic liberty and the third-base line as a scale of personal liberty. Zero on both scales was home plate. This put the conservative on first, the libertarian on second, the liberal on third, and the authoritarian at the plate. A nondescript "Centrist" occupied the pitcher's mound (see Figure 1.3).

Nolan's distinction of personal and economic freedoms suited libertarian thinking well. In the late 1970s, two political scientists, Stuart Lilie and William Maddox, applied it to surveys of voters in recent presidential

Figure 1.3
The Nolan Chart

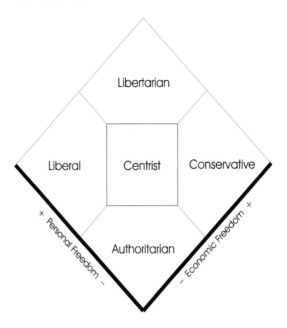

elections. Lilie and Maddox sampled responses to questions on "government intervention in economic affairs" and "expansion of personal freedoms," and then sorted voters into four categories: Conservatives, Liberals, Libertarians, and Populists (Nolan's Authoritarians).

Then, in the mid-1980s, the Nolan Chart was fitted with a survey of its own, compliments of Marshall Fritz, founder of Advocates for Self-Government. Fritz's brief ten-question quiz was meant as a marketing tool to draw attention to the chart and to popularize libertarianism. Today we can all find our place on the Nolan Chart using the on-line version of "The World's Smallest Political Quiz" at Fritz's Web site: www.self-gov.org. A similar quiz and glitzier chart, also based on the distinction between the economic and the personal, can be found at www.politopia.com, courtesy of the Institute for Humane Studies.

The Nolan Chart was a definite advance in thinking. It subjected the Right and the Left to a simple libertarian test and established the libertarian position as an independent alternative. But the chart was not without faults.

First, it does not appear that politics can be so easily divided between the personal and the economic. Take immigration, for instance. Immigration provides cheap labor, which can be good or bad depending on your *economic* perspective, but it also fuels multiculturalism, which can be good or bad depending on your *personal* perspective.

Second, the personal-versus-economic analysis overlooks the Right's preferred personal freedoms and the Left's preferred use of force to curtail them. For example, the Right wants to own guns and associate freely with whomever they wish; the Left wants to ban guns and use antidiscrimination laws and affirmative action to force us into the company of strangers. We can hardly say then that the Left stands for personal freedom.

Third, the chart is based on a libertarian definition of freedom not accepted by most liberals. Libertarians define freedom as the absence of coercion, but many on the left believe true freedom lies in having the means and opportunity to satisfy one's basic needs and desires. By this definition, economic freedom is having enough money to live as we choose, and personal freedom is not having our choices narrowed by others.

For these reasons, though still used as a teaching tool by high-school civics instructors, the Nolan Chart is not highly regarded outside libertarian circles. Its libertarian bias is too obvious. Its characterizations are too simple. Its fundamental distinction between the personal and the economic is not backed by sound theory.

LOWEST COMMON DENOMINATORS

A problem with all three schemes (Figures 1.1–1.3) is that they oppose liberty (good) to authority (bad). This is standard leftist thinking. The Right prefers to talk in terms of *power* and *authority*. It understands these as matters of *might* and *right*: Power is the *ability to compel* obedience, authority is the *right to require* it.

In the real world, however, it's not always clear where power ends and authority begins. The claim of authority itself is sometimes seen as an exercise of power. Thus we are advised to "question authority" and to beware "authoritarians." Yet no government can exist without some excuse for itself, so even antiauthoritarians claim authority for the governments they deem legitimate, distinguishing "democratic authority" from "hierarchical authority."

In *democratic* and *hierarchical* we have yet another obscuring opposition, but one which at least hints at an elemental distinction of more use to us. Democracy and hierarchy are themselves complex concepts subject to diverse interpretations, but the base of each word represents an elemental concept that Left and Right can agree on. Never mind the complicating prefixes—from *demos* meaning "people" and *hiereus* meaning "priest."

Our concern is with *archê* and *kratos*, two words often taken to mean the same thing, but which in fact represent two very different facts of life.

Archê comes from the verb *archein* meaning "to begin." The noun *archê* means beginning, origin, source, or principle, and thus also first place, top rank, sovereignty, dominion, or authority. By contrast, the Greek word *kratos* comes from the same Indo-European root as the English word *hard*. It starts out meaning bodily strength or hardiness, and later becomes strength, might, or power. In Modern Greek, *to kratos* means "the state."

For present purposes, we'll define *archê* as the concept of rank and *archy* as a ranking order. We'll define *kratos* as the use of force, especially the state's use of force. *Archê* is essentially voluntary, based as it is on each person's recognition and acceptance of rank; *kratos* is essentially involuntary, being in essence what others will do to us by force regardless of our regard for them.

Archê is essentially *personal* in that it concerns our regard for others. Do we look to other persons for our lead in life and believe ourselves to be responsible for leading others? Or do we see ourselves as morally autonomous and neither subject to nor responsible for other persons?

Kratos is essentially *political* in that it concerns the use of force—actual physical force. Governments are all about the use of force. Everything they do is backed by force. If you don't pay your taxes or your child support, the government will send men with guns to take away your property and throw you in jail.

Thus instead of might and right, we have two rights: the right to pull rank and the right to use force. Some of us believe in both, some of us believe in neither, and some of us believe in one but not the other. For example, people who accept "democratic authority" but reject "hierarchical authority" don't mind using force to get people to go along with the group, but they very much dislike recognizing a ranking order that expects them to humble themselves before someone else. Others have no problem with patriarchy, but don't believe in the government's right to coerce at all.

As it happens, this distinction of *archê* and *kratos* is not always evident. In the ancient world in particular, they often went hand in hand. Rank entailed the right to use force. The social order was coercive at all levels. There were therefore no social leaders to be distinguished from political leaders and no organized society independent of the state. Limits on *kratos* therefore necessarily entailed a limited denial of *archê*. Greek democracy and the Roman Republic were both such limited denials— they would have no kings—but both kept the archy of masters over slaves, men over women, elders over youngsters, citizens over foreigners, and patrons over clients.

Modern man has gone much further, fingering archy everywhere as the source of oppression. This is the stated understanding of the 1848 *Communist Manifesto* by Karl Marx and Friedrich Engels:

In the earlier epochs of history, we find almost everywhere a complicated arrangement of society into various orders, a manifold gradation of social rank. In ancient Rome we have patricians, knights, plebeians, slaves; in the Middle Ages, feudal lords, vassals, guild-masters, journeymen, apprentices, serfs; in almost all of these classes, again, subordinate gradations.

The modern bourgeois society that has sprouted from the ruins of feudal society has not done away with class antagonisms. It has but established new classes, new conditions of oppression, new forms of struggle in place of the old ones.

Marx and Engels proposed to end the subordination of the masses to the bourgeoisie by abolishing the basis of the bourgeoisie's power: private property. But the only way to abolish it was to counter the "social power" of the bourgeoisie with the political power of the proletariat—the *kratos* of the *demos*. On this, Marx and Engels could not be plainer. Of the Communists, the *Manifesto* declares, "They openly declare that their ends can be attained only by the *forcible* overthrow of all existing social conditions." (Emphasis added)

But how can one exercise *kratos* safely and justly without *archê*? That is the question that neither the Communists nor anyone else has ever been able to answer.

It is possible for *kratos* to exist without *archê*. A mob unorganized and leaderless can exert great force for brief moments. A small group, gang, or clique can be kept together by peer pressure and even coercion without a recognized leader. But group action over time and against resistance requires organization and direction and thus some acceptance of *archê*.

It is more common for *archê* to exist without *kratos*. All that is required is willing submission to a leader. All voluntary organizations are *akratic* by definition. Families and clans, held together by respect and affection, are akratic, though small children may need a little *kratos* now and then. Commercial corporations also are akratic: if you don't do as you are told, they stop giving you things to do and paying you for it.

This is the tyranny that Marx and Engels meant to destroy through a temporary *archê* of the proletariat, charged with abolishing not only private property, but also private education, free markets, nationhood, tradition, religion, marriage, and the family. The *Manifesto* names all these as sources of oppression. It predicts that when they are destroyed, all distinctions of class will disappear, leaving a classless society "in which the free development of each is the condition for the free development of all."

It hasn't quite worked out that way anywhere in the world, but some people today are still passionately opposed to *archê*, while others reject all use of *kratos*. The former we rightly call *anarchists*, the latter we should call *akratists*.

Anarchists are *power egalitarians*, rejecting all relationships based on dominance and submission, in which one person lords it over another, superior over subordinate, master over servant. They regard all relationships of unequal power as inherently unjust and would decide all common matters by consensus.

Akratists, on the other hand, are opposed in principle to coercion in human relations and would instead have everything managed by contract. They are not bothered by the master/servant relationship as long as it is based on a freely made contract. They even reject the state's claim to sovereignty over people and property, absent a contract with all involved parties, a contract that any party can opt out of if need be.

It happens that these two contrarians—the anarchist and the akratist—are found only in the West, for only the West has given people the choice of rejecting *archê* or *kratos*, or both, or neither. It did this by separating its sources of *archê* and *kratos* organizationally, entrusting *kratos* to the state but seeking its source of *archê* in the Christian Church. Only Christian civilization has known this complication of a separate, independent, archical organization of society to stand beside or against the political organization of the state. And only when the West began to turn away from the institutional Church did the peculiar complexity of Western political thinking arise.

POLITICS IN THE AGE OF ANARCHY

The modern age might well be called the Age of Anarchy. It began around 1500 with a rebellion against hierarchy (the rule of priests), which led in time to a rebellion against monarchy (the rule of kings) and culminated in our own day with a rebellion against patriarchy (the rule of men, of fathers, and of God the Father). All along, however, the rebels have tended to confuse issue of *archê* with the issue of *kratos*. Only by distinguishing the two can we untangle the threads of history to make more sense of our distinctively Western political complexity.

For over a thousand years, church and state coexisted in a sometimes uneasy partnership, according to what was known in the Christian West as the Two Swords doctrine and in the Byzantine East as the ideal of *symphonia.* This partnership limited the role of the state in society's affairs, leaving many matters of public good to the Church.

The Protestant Reformation, however, laid the axe to the root of the Church's archic power, exalting the individual believer against the church hierarchy and promoting a passionate repudiation of personal authority and subjection. This greatly weakened the Western Church, undermining its standing vis-à-vis the state and freeing the state to take full control.

These two crosswise currents—rebellious individualism and political absolutism—account for the confused course of Western political development. The history of the West is often presented as the steady ascent of freedom out of medieval oppression, when in fact the collapse of the Christian consensus on politics brought violent swings between freedom and tyranny, with demands for utter allegiance to the State contending against an implacable passion for rebellion.

Now, by distinguishing *archê* and *kratos*, we can trace the four divergent political traditions of the Anglo-American experience. Three of these traditions arose out of the liberal or "whig" reaction to the growth of the centralized, absolutized, national state; the fourth tradition arose out of the struggle by the commercial might of the national state to maintain its dominance.

The first tradition was *republican constitutionalism*, which accepted traditional social *archê* but resisted the often anti-traditional *kratos* of the modern state. This tradition arose in England as an attempt to preserve traditional limits to the royal prerogative based on feudal rights, English common law, and the Britain's "Ancient Constitution." It looked to the past, to a legal tradition based on custom and precedent and not on the will of an official lawgiver. It retained the medieval understanding of divided and limited sovereignty, upheld by the primacy of law over power, right over might. The sovereign was seen as subject to the laws of the land and thus not entirely free to rule arbitrarily. The challenge was to find a secure basis for limited government in the absence of a church to counterbalance the state. Various schemes were put forth to limit the power of the monarch, the military, and the monied interests. The common concern was a conservative one—preserving the order and liberty to which they were accustomed against an expansive central power.[3]

The second tradition was *libertarian individualism*, which resisted both social *archê* and political *kratos*. This tradition regarded precedent and authority with less respect and made claims of new rights and liberties for individuals, on the basis of a transcendent authority known only through faith or reason. Such thinking owed much to Protestant belief in free association, individual autonomy, social contract, and the right of resistance to unjust authority. It gave rise to quasi-libertarian notions of individual rights that a man can only surrender freely or forfeit by misdemeanor. John Locke's (1632–1704) contribution was to rationalize many radical notions such as the state of nature, the consent of the governed, and natural rights. The state of nature denied any natural subordination of individuals to family, clan, class, or community. The consent of the governed invalidated both Divine Right and Ancient Constitutions. Natural rights—when assumed to be inalienable and self-evident, and therefore unarguable—insulated the individual from all outside authority, thus making the individual himself the ground of truth and basis of justice.[4]

The third tradition was *progressive democracy*, which rejected social *archê* but did not shrink from the use of political *kratos*. This tradition replaced the absolute sovereignty of the King with the absolute sovereignty of Parliament and later the People. It was less concerned for individual rights and liberties than for social equality and progress. It identified tyranny with the social archy of feudal rank, material inequality, and clerical authority. It would seek deliverance in popular governance, communal equality, and freedom from tradition. Progressive democracy's chief prophet was Jean-Jacques Rousseau (1712–1778). Rousseau delivered a sweeping condemnation of the existing order, blaming private property and the resulting inequality for corrupting and enslaving the civilized world. He declared that people were naturally good and only made bad by civilization. Their natural goodness made them capable of democratic governance once civilization's old, corrupting, superstitious, hierarchical institutions were swept away. All that the people needed was an enlightened lawgiver to help them identify their "general will" and even force them to be free if need be. Rousseau let it known that he was at their service.[5]

The fourth tradition was *plutocratic nationalism*, which accepted both social *archê* and political *kratos* as beneficial facts of life. This tradition was rooted in the "new absolutism" of the post-Reformation period, in which national monarchs claimed unlimited sovereignty based on Divine Right, against the Church's claim of partnership and the customary restraints of the feudal system.[6] In England, after the English Civil War, this power was transferred to the national government headed by a constitutional monarch but administered by a parliament organized by wealthy lords representing the nation's dominant financial interests. After the American Revolution, a similar system formed the basis of Alexander Hamilton's High Federalism. Hamilton wanted a strong national government, headed by a strong chief executive, backed by a central bank, and empowered to levy protective tariffs and fund internal improvements like roads and canals to benefit commerce and industry.[7]

The American colonists drew on the first three traditions to justify the cause of independence. They claimed a political autonomy consistent with medieval notions of divided sovereignty or "empire within empire." They claimed the protection of Britain's Ancient Constitution. They claimed inalienable rights conferred on individual men by God. They claimed popular sovereignty, damning all kings as tyrants.[8] It was an odd mixture that succeeded nowhere else but in America. But there it did succeed by drawing all the sundry sons of liberty together in the common cause.

Union after independence was another matter, over which the sons of liberty had their first falling out. In the debates over the Articles of Confederation, the fourth tradition reasserted itself, prompting the adoption of the federal Constitution. Afterward the four traditions continued in contention, each claiming a corner of the American political mind.

All four of these traditions are still quite with us. All four are modern in origin, though some show more respect toward the past than others. All four are "post-Christian" in the sense that none provides an equal role for an established church as a full partner of the state. All four have at different times laid claim to the name of *liberal.* Each still considers itself the best friend of true freedom, and each can be sorted easily to the left or the right of the graphical scheme we will now construct.

Chapter 2

Beyond Left and Right

This alone I have found, that God, when he made man, made him straightforward, but man invents endless subtleties of his own.

Ecclesiastes 7:29

As it happens, our conventional distinction of Left and Right is mostly a matter of *archê* and not *kratos*. We will therefore follow convention and use a horizontal axis as the scale of *archê*—archy to the right, anarchy to the left. We'll then add a vertical axis as the scale of *kratos*. This being the Land of the Free, we'll make the point of maximum *kratos* the bottom of this axis and label the top *akrateia* (the absence of *kratos*).

We now have a place to put our four divergent political traditions. Our *progressive democrats*, who resist *archê* but do not shrink from the use of *kratos*, belong in the lower left. Our *republican constitutionalists*, who accept *archê* but resist *kratos*, belong in the upper right. Our *libertarian individualists*, who resist both *archê* and *kratos*, belong in the upper left. Our *plutocratic nationalists*, who accept and embrace both *archê* and *kratos*, belong in the lower right.

Remember that *Republican* and *Democrat* in Figure 2.1 mean two of the four main Anglo-American political traditions, not today's Republican and Democratic parties, though the parties' choice of names is not entirely accidental. Today's Democratic Party does descend from the democratic tradition, though for much of its history the party also attracted individualists and republicans. On the other hand, the Republican Party, for much of its history, represented the plutocratic nationalists of the lower right, attracting individualists and republicans only later in reaction to democratic dominance.

Figure 2.1
Four Political Americans

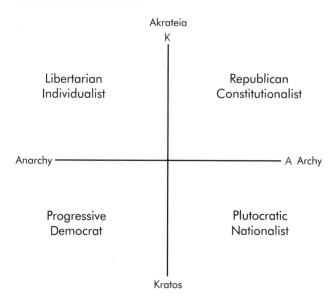

Akrateia
K

Libertarian   Republican
Individualist   Constitutionalist

Anarchy ──────────────┼────────────── A Archy

Progressive   Plutocratic
Democrat   Nationalist

Kratos

Many historians have tried to fit the political history of the United States into the narrative of a single authentically American tradition. More recently, historians have acknowledged more diverse contributions to American politics. Figure 2.1 brings order to this diversity, helping to explain the many shifts in American politics as the continuing contention of four main traditions. Most of the time, this contention has pitted the lower right against a coalition of the other quadrants. In recent years, however, a coalition of the lower right and the upper quadrants has checked the power of the lower left. The new coalition is represented by the Republican Party, the party of the "Big Tent." The lower left is the sole preserve of the Democratic Party.

We will revisit the dynamics of shifting power in the last chapter. For now, let's look closer at the familiar distinction of Left and Right, using our A and K axes to explain it.

THE ESSENCE OF LEFT AND RIGHT

The Left in Figure 2.1 is not defined by its regard for government, but by its rejection of archy, especially patriarchy. Both individualists and democrats are anarchists in that they deny the existence of a natural order setting one over another. Both also follow Rousseau in believing that man is basically good, though they differ on what this means. To the individualist, it means that individuals can be trusted with freedom; to the democrat, it means that the people can be trusted with power. Individualists and democrats differ most in their regard for government and in their emphasis on private versus public interests. One would minimize government and maximize personal freedom, with little concern for inequality; the other would use government to achieve as much equality as possible.

The Right is defined by its acceptance of a naturally archical order in society. Both plutocrats and republicans believe that man, if not basically bad, is nevertheless certainly fallen, and therefore requires restraint. They differ, however, on who needs restraint most. The plutocrat is most concerned to restrain the rabble below him; the republican is most concerned to restrain the bigwigs above him. The former would strengthen the central power to keep order against the pressures of anarchic individualism; the latter would limit the central power to keep local life free from progressive lawgivers. The plutocrat looks to the central government to rationalize society for the sake of order and efficiency; the republican looks to families, churches, and local authorities to conserve a natural and traditional society, free of outside interference.

The groups that matter most to the Right are inherently archical and paternal: family and church for republicans, commercial corporations and government itself for plutocrats. Among government agencies, the Right is more inclined to trust rank-conscious agencies like the military and the police, and the executive branch in general.

By contrast, the Left is more at ease with the free-for-all of democratic politics and less comfortable with archical agencies, which it disdains as authoritarian. The Left avoids archy through personal independence and anarchical associations. The latter are either mutual arrangements between individuals (as between buyers and sellers, or between domestic partners) or broad classes of people with common interests but no archical structure (women, minorities, the working class, etc.).

It is the Left's rejection of archy *but not politics* that makes Western political thinking distinctive. All other civilizations have regarded the rejection of archy as the ultimate rebellion and marked the anarchist as an antisocial outlaw: All such civilizations had only the choice of the upper left and the lower right, a simple trade-off between freedom and order, between the interests of the individual and the good of the group.

In the West, however, the identification of the governing *archê* with a separate institution, the Christian Church, seemed to allow the option of rejecting the justification of social rank without destroying the basis of

Figure 2.2
The Eight Ways

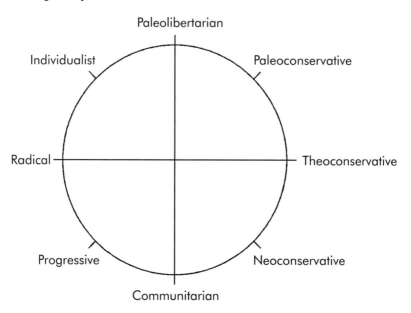

social order. Westerners were tempted to believe that anarchy need not mean chaos, that people can live together in organized communities and yet remain individually free, with no one subject to anyone else.

THE EIGHT WAYS

Now, at last, we are ready to take the final step and apply our scheme to the contemporary American political scene. It happens that as our four main traditions diverge, four distinct intermediate perspectives emerge. We'll plot all eight perspectives around a circle to form the compass in Figure 2.2. The following chapters will study each of these perspectives in detail. For now, let's take a look at a thumbnail sketch of each, starting with perhaps the easiest to understand, at the bottom of the K axis.

The Communitarian

The Communitarian is a pragmatist and a technocrat whose focus is always on the good of the community, hence the name. Since the political order is now the only order representing the whole community, the Communitarian's focus is naturally political. As for the social powers of church and family, the Communitarian values their contribution to a healthy, orderly society, but he tends to see them as parts of the whole, constituent members of society needing support and encouragement, and sometimes regulation.

The Communitarian will concede for the sake of argument that government can't do everything; he will even admit when pressed that government is sometimes part of the problem; but he can't help but think that government is often also a big part of the solution. The Communitarian is always hopeful that some new policy or program will solve the problem at hand. If it doesn't, he thinks first of giving it more money, more time, or more teeth (i.e., more *kratos*). Only when the evidence of failure is overwhelming will the Communitarian give up—and start looking for another new government policy or program to take its place.

The Communitarian fears neither excessive size nor centralization. On the contrary, he sees bigness and centralization as good because they strengthen the hand administering the medicine. True federalism, with its arbitrary reservations of powers, goes against his nature. Leaving important matters such as education and health care to state and local governments— or, worse, to the market—is shamefully irresponsible to the Communitarian.

The Communitarian sees himself as sensibly middle-of-the-road, a moderate betwixt unreasonable ideologues. He does indeed lie midway on the A axis, equidistant from the Progressives on his left and the Neoconservatives on his right. But he's a lot closer to the lower left than to the upper right, and so his policies are almost always more appealing to Progressives than to Paleoconservatives. The Communitarian regards most everyone else around the circle as extreme and unhelpful. He seeks the common good and complains of excessive individualism and ideology. We suffer, he believes, from a selfish assertion of individual rights and special interests that all too often trump the rights and needs of the community. What is needed is more balance between the two.

Governments under Communitarians tend to grow, having little reason not to. Hope springs eternal for the Communitarian's many problem-solving programs, for without an antigovernment principle in his philosophy, the Communitarian can't easily tell where the limits of government should be.

The Paleolibertarian

If the Communitarian is a left-leaning statist, his exact opposite must be a right-leaning libertarian. A few years back, some such creatures took the name *paleolibertarian* to distinguish themselves from the left-leaning libertarians of the Libertarian Party. We'll use Paleolibertarian, too, and its short form—Paleolib.

Like the Communitarian, the Paleolib sees the world chiefly in political terms, but whereas the Communitarian lacks an antigovernment principle, the Paleolib lacks a pro-government principle: At its best, government is a necessary evil; at its worst, it is the greatest evil the world has ever known. This extremely negative view is encouraged by the progressive tendencies of modern governments, which the Paleolib blames for many crimes committed against Christian civilization.

If not an outright akratist (or "anarcho-capitalist"), the Paleolib is at least an extreme decentralist. He sees the greatest threat coming from the highest levels of government, the furthest removed from real life. He would gladly abolish much of the modern federal government. All of the proud achievements of twentieth century would go—the Great Society, the New Frontier, the New Deal, the Federal Reserve, and the federal income tax, which pays for them all. Even at the lower levels, the Paleolib would trim government back to bare bone, mostly by abolishing the public school system. He would also repeal antidiscrimination laws on principle, seeing them as infringements on property rights, contract law, and the freedoms of speech and association, all of which are important preconditions of a free market.

While always darkly critical of existing governments, the Paleolib is confident of man's ability to live without government. He believes that virtually everything that governments have tried to manage—from lighthouses to law enforcement—can be better managed by private persons or groups. The Paleolib's singular focus on the evils of government leads him to place great emphasis on private associations, at least in theory. He tends, however, to see no possibility of cooperation between social and political powers. The two are either in conflict or in danger of one corrupting the other through the use of *kratos* for the wrong purposes.

The Paleolib is therefore inclined against using force to defend traditional religion and morality. Although close to the Paleoconservative in overall outlook, the Paleolib trusts that the social order will not need defending once the threat of government is removed.

The Theoconservative

At the far right of the A axis is another animal altogether. Unlike both the Paleolib and the Communitarian, the Theoconservative does not see more or less government as society's biggest problem or best solution. He is more concerned about the social institutions that to him actually are society: family, church, neighborhood, company, and community.

The Theocon's focus is naturally personal and local, and so for a long time Theocons did not take an active role in politics. That changed in the 1970s, as the personal became increasingly political. Theocons have since become very involved, though always somewhat uneasily. The trouble, as they see it, is the breakdown of the social order as a result of the waning influence of the traditional social powers of church and family. The real remedy, they believe, is a revival of faith, both at home and in the halls of power.

The Theocon's first allegiance is to God; toward Caesar, he is ambivalent. On one hand, he believes that government is ordained by God and naturally looks with respect on higher authorities. On the other hand, he is fearful of state interference in church and family matters and alarmed by the State's alignment against traditional morality. He is also uncomfortable with politics, which he regards as dangerously worldly and distracting from the things that matter most.

The Theocon desires not so much a state religion as a religious state, in which faith is strong and the church is honored, influential, and independent. Otherwise, the Theocon's political philosophy is rather vague and very American. He does not question the country's founding principles, but he interprets them in Christian ways, emphasizing the country's Christian roots. He sees America as originally a God-favored nation and worries that it has turned its back on God.

The Theocon is not a state-hater dreaming of a world without the Federal Reserve. He favors stability in politics and government and faithfulness to familiar political procedures and institutions. He picks and chooses the policies he supports according to their impact on faith and family. Policies that encourage faith and strengthen the family are good; policies that discourage faith and weaken the family are bad. Prayer in public schools is good; sex education in public schools is bad.

To the Communitarian and the Paleolib, the Theocon is inconsistent in his application of *kratos*. But from his own perspective, he is entirely consistent, always placing first things first: faith and family before politics.

The Radical

At the opposite end of the A axis is the Radical. A rebel by nature, the Radical is constitutionally averse to tradition and archy, whether religious, familial, commercial, or political. He questions authority, loathes the military, and hates the corporations, which he believes really run things.

The Radical is deeply dissatisfied with the world as it is. He longs for a simpler time when humankind tread lightly upon the earth in harmonious, egalitarian communities, somewhat resembling extended families but without the curse of patriarchy. He believes that sin entered the world when the first few selfish men conspired to fence off private lots, enslave their fellow humans, and despoil the environment to satisfy their own greed.

At the heart of the Radical's thinking is his belief in the good nature and cooperative spirit of all people when not threatened with coercion. With Rousseau, the Radical believes that all social ills are the result of oppression—one man dominating another. The Radical's solution to this problem of dominance is to reorder society in ways that eliminate the need for archy. The Radical seeks a society governed entirely by consensus, in which everyone has a full and equal say.

Today, the Radical's chief villains are the great, heartless, mercenary, patriarchal, transnational corporations bent on globalizing (commercializing) the planet. Toward government, the Radical is deeply ambivalent. He turns to government to serve and protect the people and the environment from corporate greed, but he recoils from the archical form that government tends to take. He always suspects that the dreaded corporations have secretly rigged "the system" to their own advantage, buying off venal politicians with hefty campaign donations. The Radical longs for the return of true democracy, in which everyone has a say, no matter who they are or how much money they have.

Like the Theocon, the Radical justifies the use of force by its ends. If it frees us from the tyranny of tradition, greed, and archy, it is good; if it strengthens the hand of the repressive social or commercial order, it is bad. Prayer in public schools is bad, but sex education in the same schools is good. Campaign finance reform is good, but "censorship" in public funding of the arts is bad. Again, the inconsistency exists only for the more politically minded, who see the world quite differently than both the Theocon and the Radical.

The Individualist

In between the Radical and the Paleolibertarian, we have another kind of libertarian, who is really more of an Individualist.

The Individualist's view of the world is less political than the Paleolib's. While the Paleolib might describe his position as "us against the State," the Individualist is more likely to describe his position as "me against the world." He feels equally threatened by both social and political pressures. He is deeply resentful of people trying to "impose their morality" on others.

He chafes within archical organizations and prefers independence and self-employment when he can get them. He is pro-progress, anti-tradition, and often anti-Christian. He is often a rationalist and a materialist and is sometimes an "Objectivist" disciple of Ayn Rand.

The Individualist's sense of justice is fundamentally individualistic, with heavy emphasis on individual rights and liberties. For this reason, the Individualist is often not as antigovernment as the Paleolib. He is not without a pro-government principle: government exists to protect the rights of individuals and enforce contracts between them. In contrast to the Paleolib's insistence on decentralization, the Individualist often looks to higher levels of government to keep the lower levels in check, using federal law and federal judges to curb excesses of state and local power. He is extra sensitive to threats to civil liberties, but less bothered than the Paleolib by antidiscrimination laws. His solution to the problem of dominance is to enlist government in the service of individual rights.

The Individualist is a fierce defender of property rights and the free market. He has more hope for capitalism than democracy, seeing democracy as a potential threat to individual liberty and capitalism as the surest means of satisfying his own desires and breaking down social and political restraints. He favors legalization of victimless crimes such as prostitution and recreational use of narcotics, both because he resents such restrictions on private behavior and because he fears the police measures used to enforce them.

Despite the continuing growth of government, at home and abroad, the Individualist is brightly optimistic about the future. Always individual in his focus, he is less concerned about the weight of government on society than about its weight upon himself. As long as he remains free to pursue his own happiness and achieve his own self-actualization, he is not alarmed.

The Neoconservative

"Neoconservatism" is a relatively new name but not a new view. At its base is a belief in a strong central government to defend the established order, with all necessary cooperation between the social and political powers—church and state, business and government. The former liberals who were the first to bear the name *neoconservative* migrated to this view but did not originate it. They did, however, provide it with the intellectual respectability the lower right has long lacked.

Neoconservatism is "neo" in its embrace of democratic capitalism and American melting-pot pluralism; it is "conservative" in its rejection of democratic socialism and anti-Western multiculturalism. The Neocon's chief concern is the health of our modern, wealth-creating, pluralistic capitalist state, which the Neocon sees as threatened from within by the burden of government on business (excessive taxation and regulation) and by the corruption of conventional bourgeois values, upon which democracy and capitalism depend. He sees the state as threatened from without by militant Islam and rival nations like Russia and China.

The Neocon would shift some public responsibilities to the private sector and use the private sector to accomplish public aims. He typically supports national education standards, federal funding for local schools and faith-based social programs, and conservative use of federal funds for the arts and humanities. He would even support tighter restrictions on pornography, compulsory national service, and an end to affirmative action if such things were politically possible. Believing they are not, he doesn't waste much capital on them.

On many controversial social issues like abortion, affirmative action, and gay rights, the Neocon limits himself to guerrilla tactics, sniping at the Left on the general issues while avoiding showdowns over actual policy. This strategy does not sit well with other conservatives who see the sniping as grandstanding and the avoidance as evidence of insincerity. To such critics, Neocons seem too often to be giving ground even while advancing their own interests.

The Neocon is, above all, a political realist intent on actually winning and keeping control of government. He therefore favors an incremental approach to turning the ship of state around, advocating limited reforms like tax cuts, school choice, and partial privatization of Social Security. His devotion to capitalism makes him often an ally of the Individualist, but the Neocon's perspective on capitalism is more corporatist than individualist. A libertarian will argue laissez-faire because he distrusts big government; the Neocon will argue deregulation because he trusts big business.

The Paleoconservative

The Paleoconservative descends from a long line of American defenders of traditional values and limited government, but the name itself is even newer than *neoconservative*. In fact, the *paleo* prefix was adopted by a handful of traditional conservatives in the 1980s to distinguish themselves from the neoconservatives who had edged them out of influence in the Reagan administration. Our use of Paleocon here includes many traditional conservatives who were not caught up in the paleo/neo rift, but are often classed as traditionalists.

Whereas the Neocon's view is more political and economic, and the Theocon's view is more social and religious, the Paleocon's view is more historical and cultural. He is less accepting of conventional American historiography and more inclined to look beyond the American experience to its English and European roots. He puts less stock in vague universal values like freedom, democracy, capitalism, and human rights; he puts more stock in particular distinctions among people like language, religion, gender, ethnicity, nationality, and race.

The Paleocon believes in free enterprise, but he is suspicious of business and government working too closely together. He is especially alarmed by antidiscrimination laws, which subsume the business world into the coercive political order, in effect deputizing corporations to enforce official orthodoxy. The Paleocon is also quite critical of the modern world's selfish consumerism. He is sympathetic to environmental concerns but not to the nature worship of the environmental movement. He sometimes waxes nostalgic for the chivalrous agrarian culture of the antebellum South and typically sides with the South on states' rights and secession, against the crass commercialism and romantic moralism of the crusading North.

Politically, the Paleocon is a citizen of the Old Republic. He wants a return to the truly federal form of government that reserved for the States and the People more freedom and power. He shares the Paleolib's antigovernment animus, but not his unlimited faith in freedom or the libertarian rationalization of individualism. He would adopt many of the Paleolib's proposals for dismantling the modern, bureaucratic, regulatory federal government, but he would be more inclined than the Paleolib to favor local laws to protect public health and morals.

The Progressive

The Paleocon's exact opposite is the Progressive, to whom change is good, new is better, progress is inevitable, and "traditional" is a multipurpose pejorative applied to anything they don't like anymore. The distance between the Paleocon and the Progressive is the measure of movement in Western culture over the last several centuries—away from a world governed by fathers, priests, and local lords according to Christian faith and ancient custom, toward a world governed by the People acting through public officials according to universal values of progress, tolerance, inclusiveness, and equality.

The Progressive solves the problem of dominance by redistributing wealth, power, and privilege from the haves to the have-nots. By thus eliminating the inequalities of condition, the Progressive hopes to avoid not the organizational archy that exists in all governing structures, but the class archy that empowers one group of people to impose its values on other groups. The Progressive is often quite keen on governing structures, as long as they are democratic, meaning that they are accountable to the "will of the People," the only authority the Progressive recognizes.

The Progressive shares the Radical's leftist social orientation but not his aversion to government. He is more at ease with power and less paranoid of its uses. The Radical is a rebel; the Progressive is a reformer. Rads agitate; Progs legislate. Rads drop out; Progs sell out (if you believe the Rads). Where the Radical sees swelling corruption, the Progressive sees a march of progress, out of the Dark Age and into the New Age.

Progressives are confident that the human condition can be infinitely improved if we just keep trying. They are also quite impatient with those who believe that human nature is fixed and fallen and that archy and inequality are therefore both inescapable and necessary. In matters of morality, the Progressive is a relativist, except when it comes to the injustice of class archy, which the Progressive sees as a simple matter of certain people victimizing certain other people.

For many years, Progressives focused on economics as the source and solution to society's problems. Today, they are still inclined to try to manage the economy, though most have grudgingly given up on central planning. Their focus is now on making capitalism socially responsible and on fixing the political system so as to shift power to the powerless and advantage to the disadvantaged.

We are now ready to take a closer look at each of our eight perspectives. But before going further, let's note two general observations about our Compass.

The first observation is that the Compass actually allows for a ninth perspective in the center of the circle. This is the true centrist, but he is more recognizable by the name *populist*. Populism has no constant character except general dissatisfaction with the status quo (political or cultural) among people out of power whose social and political views are not well defined. This dissatisfaction is often based on a feeling that something fundamental is wrong with the modern world, but it is often expressed popularly as a complaint that government isn't working or is doing too much or too little. Such complaints can be heard every day, but in a crisis they can grow to great volume and call forth a leader to rally the people against the ruling powers. The crisis and the leader decide the character of the movement, whether it will be conservative or progressive, antigovernment or anticorporation. Almost always, the crisis passes, the leader fades, and the followers give up politics or are pulled to the periphery, often in different directions.

The second observation is that the three perspectives at the bottom of the Compass are typically more pragmatic than the others. This follows from their interest in political power, which forces them to think practically about what works to give them power and how to use it most effectively. The other five perspectives are not so concerned with getting power and are therefore typically more idealistic, more concerned with the way things should be than with the way they can win. One consequence of this difference is that the bottom three win more often. Another consequence is that the bottom three are more restrained in revealing their dreamier ambitions, while the upper five feel freer to carry their thinking, good or bad, to its logical extremes. Thus it sometimes seems that all "extremists" are on top, but this is not so, as we shall see.

Chapter 3

For Common Things: The Communitarian

Hearken not to the unnatural voice which tells you that the people of America, knit together as they are by so many cords of affection, can no longer live together as members of the same family; can no longer continue the mutual guardians of their mutual happiness; can no longer be fellow-citizens of one great, respectable, and flourishing empire.

James Madison
The Federalist, No. 14, 1787

They are less and less political decisions, more and more administrative ones. They are decisions that can be reached by consensus rather than conflict.

Daniel Patrick Moynihan
Miles to Go: A Personal History of Social Policy, 1996

Michael Lind was raised in Texas as a New Deal Democrat. Then he went to Yale, where he met "left-liberalism in all of its folly and fury." Lind's "Humphrey-Johnson Democratic liberalism" earned him a reputation for conservatism: "I concluded that the vital center of American politics was more likely to be restored by the center-right than by the center-left." He remained a Democrat, but began to think of himself as a "neoconservative." He went to work for the Heritage Foundation. He was hired as a research assistant to William F. Buckley Jr. He got a grant from conservative godfather Russell Kirk to write a book on political theory. Before long, he was managing editor of Irving Kristol's *The National Interest*.

Then in 1990, President George Bush broke his no-new-taxes pledge, and Lind was forced to rethink his allegiances once again:

I could not understand why the conservatives were pouring derision on President Bush for his decision to cooperate with Congress in raising taxes to reduce the deficit. By that time, after all, it should have been clear to any intelligent person that "Reaganomics" had been discredited. Much to my astonishment, supply-side economics not only rose from the dead but became the orthodoxy once again on the right.[1]

The final straw came in 1992, when the same President Bush welcomed Patrick J. Buchanan to his side at the Republican National Convention after Buchanan's infamous "culture war" speech. This was Lind's epiphany:

There, on the national level, was the alliance of callous plutocracy and crackpot fundamentalism that was the basis of the classical Texan and Southern conservatism that I had grown up despising—an alliance which I had hoped that a more centrist, inclusive national conservative movement had forever left behind.[2]

Take out Texas and Lind could easily serve as the archetypal moderate idealist caught in a tug-of-war between Left and Right, struggling to define himself by transcending the contest. Over the years, such idealists have assumed many names: moderates, centrists, new conservatives, neoconservatives, neoprogressives, neoliberals, national liberals, communitarians, the Vital Center, the Radical Center, and the Third Way. Their common values are pragmatism, moderation, national unity, strong central government, innovative and experimental policymaking, putting common interests over individual rights, seeking consensus instead of conflict, for the good of all.

What to call them? We could call them moderates or centrists, but they aren't really either except in relation to Progressives and Neoconservatives, which are for them the only other respectable positions. We could call them technocrats or bureaucrats, given their wonkish fondness for public policy and faith in government fixes, but neither name really gets at what these folks are all about. Their concern is not just policy or government, or even mere moderation. Their concern is the national and international community, and so we will call them communitarians. Not everyone who goes by the name belongs in this camp, but many leading communitarians do. Our Compass helps us see why.

Communitarians see themselves as the sensible alternative to all ideological extremes. They are not entirely nonideological, but they are less ideological and more pragmatic than everyone else around the Compass. They want what is right for all concerned, and what is right can only be what works.

A good example is the late Senator Daniel Patrick Moynihan of New York. The son of working-class immigrants, a beneficiary of the New Deal and G.I. Bill, Moynihan took the pragmatic approach to public policy and the general welfare, seeking better policy through empirical research. "The central political issue of most industrial nations over the past century and a half has been how to make an economy work," he wrote in his 1996 memoir *Miles to Go.* "The industrial nations of the world seem finally about to learn how to manage their economies." Economics "is becoming an applied science."[3]

Moynihan held senior positions in two moderate Republican administrations, those of Presidents Nixon and Ford, but he was never much a part of either party until he decided to run for office. He picked the Democratic Party partly because it offered the best chances in his home state of New York. He was generally loyal to the party throughout his career, but he was never entirely trusted by the party's Progressives and Radicals. He was too close to the circle of New York intellectuals calling themselves "neoconservatives," though he never moved far enough into the lower right to qualify as a Neoconservative for our purposes. He was a Cold War hero as ambassador to the United Nations, but showed little interest in foreign policy after the Cold War's close. Social issues concerned him more, and on them he was an old-fashioned liberal. Though generally pro-choice, he likened partial-birth abortion to infanticide and voted to ban it. He backed privatization of Social Security, but vigorously opposed the 1996 welfare reform. He publicly criticized President Clinton's behavior, but argued against removing him from office, prompting Christopher Hitchens to write, "Senator Daniel Patrick Moynihan, as so often, provided the fluid pivot and axis on which such a strategy could be made to turn, according to need, or according to the needs of New York's lumpen intellectuals."[4]

Such pivoting could be explained as political expedience, but for Communitarians pivoting is an essential talent and an honorable exercise. The problem is how to justify it, which intellectual Communitarians keep trying to do.

Political centrism first arose as a distinct alternative in American politics after World War II, in reaction to the Democratic Left's benign regard for Soviet Communism. Worried liberals like Arthur Schlesinger, author of *The Vital Center*, tried to define a third position that was pro-New Deal, pro-Cold War, and not too anti-business. The rise of the antiestablishment New Left in the 1960s exacerbated centrist concerns. After the McGovernite takeover of the Democratic Party in 1972, centrist Democrats formed the Coalition for a Democratic Majority. But the Democratic Party's long march to the left soon turned many CDM Democrats into neoconservative Republicans.

Some of the centrists who stayed with the Democratic Party formed the Democratic Leadership Council (DLC) in 1984. Derided by party leftists as "Democrats Looking for Cash," the DLC nevertheless helped its chairman, Bill Clinton, win the White House in 1992. But this success did less to build a centrist consensus in the Democratic Party than to rally the party's Progressive center, which had been on the ropes during the Reagan years. Consequently, after eight more years, a new centrist group rose on the DLC's right called the Project for Conservative Reform, a John McCain-inspired group of "Progressive Republicans" bridging Communitarianism and Neoconservatism.

Such centrism is often a pragmatic bid for electoral victory. On the Left, John B. Judis and Ruy Teixeira, authors of *The Emerging Democratic Majority*, write hopefully of an emerging "progressive center" in between the Great Society and laissez faire, drawing strength from the swelling ranks of women, minorities, and professionals, but threatened by ideological impatience:

If the Democrats move too quickly to embrace the culture of the new Bohemia— say, by pressing civil unions or gun prohibition—they could lose much of their still-vital, white, working-class support. . . . But as long as the Democrats maintain a fiscally moderate, socially liberal, reformist, and egalitarian outlook, they will enjoy a structural edge in national and most state elections.[5]

Such centrism is a tactic, its moderation merely a mask for an ideology unappealing at present to a voting majority. It is not true centrism, neither is it Communitarianism.

Communitarian centrism is less tactical and more personal. The true Communitarian is sincere in his distaste for conflict and genuinely distressed by the divisiveness and polarization in our society, which he blames on ideological extremes. As he sees it, progress could have proceeded smoothly and sensibly, but the Left became impatient and unreasonable, and the Right responded with reaction and regression. The nation's natural evolution was interrupted by a bitter culture war that has confused the issues and obstructed necessary adaptions to changing technological and demographic circumstances.

This is the view outlined by E.J. Dionne Jr. in his 1991 book *Why Americans Hate Politics*: "The New Left became antidemocratic and highly destructive. It polarized American life around false issues and false choices. In ways it did not intend, the New Left also played a decisive role in undermining liberalism's influence on American life." Dionne quotes Schlesinger's definition of democracy as "the search for remedy." The problem is that ideologues on both sides have abandoned the search and pursued their own narrow agendas. What's needed, says Dionne, is a return to the "politics of remedy" with more emphasis on common values and common interests: "We are encouraging either/or politics based on ideological preconceptions rather than a 'both/and' politics based on ideas that broadly unite us."[6]

The "politics of remedy" explains the Communitarians' preoccupation with technocratic fixes for perceived problems. Communitarians are policy wonks by nature. They are never bored by detailed discussions of public policy. Often their interests strike others as off the wall. The day before the September 11 terrorist attacks on the World Trade Center and the Pentagon, the cover story of the DLC's *Blueprint* magazine warned of a "mobility crisis" threatening America due to a lack of public transportation. Timing aside, only a Communitarian would be so alarmed by the lack of public transportation as to call it a crisis.

But Communitarians aren't just policy wonks. Their policy preferences are carefully balanced to help us escape the distraction of ideology and unite behind our common interests, like balancing rights and responsibilities, strengthening basic moral values, providing equal opportunity without demanding equal outcomes, ensuring personal and national security, exercising fiscal discipline, adapting government regulation and the social safety net to the New Economy, and building a new global system based on democracy, human rights, and economic prosperity.

Such concerns are the basis of the Third Way, as defined by the Progressive Policy Institute (PPI), the DLC's own think tank. PPI names the Third Way's "three cornerstones" equal opportunity (but not special privileges), mutual responsibility (neither entitlement nor abandonment), and self-government (not personal freedom, as libertarians would define it, but providing choices and empowering citizens to act on them). In other words:

The Third Way approach to economic opportunity and security stresses technological innovation, competitive enterprise, and education rather than top-down redistribution or laissez faire. On questions of values, it embraces "tolerant traditionalism," honoring traditional moral and family values while resisting attempts to impose them on others. It favors an enabling rather than a bureaucratic government, expanding choices for citizens, using market means to achieve public ends and encouraging civic and community institutions to play a larger role in public life. The Third Way works to build inclusive, multiethnic societies based on common allegiance to democratic values.[7]

Michael Lind and Ted Halstead sound many of these same notes in their 2001 book *The Radical Center*. Halstead is the founder and president of the New America Foundation, the latest organized attempt to define an independent center against the left and right wings. Lind is a senior fellow at New America. (Jedediah Purdy, author of *For Common Things*, is a fellow.)

New America is, in Halstead's words, "beyond left and right." *The Radical Center* explains what he means. Echoing Dionne, Halstead and Lind blame our current ideological deadlock on a "three-decade eruption of narrow particularism—featuring the identity-group politics of the multicultural Left and the religious Right, and the libertarian glorification of the market above all other sectors of society." The result, they say, is the "illusion of a sharply divided nation" and a "two-party duopoly" that cannot bring America together because each party has been "captured by their extremes."[8]

As an alternative, Halstead and Lind offer the Radical Center, a quasi-populist Newer New Deal for the twenty-first century. Democratic liberalism and Republican conservatism are "vestiges of the Second Industrial Revolution"; the Radical Center is designed for the Information Age. It is neither traditional nor revolutionary, but evolutionary and reformist: "The great civic reformers of the American past changed what was ephemeral and secondary in the American tradition in order to conserve what was permanent and important." Halstead and Lind promise that the Radical Center will do the same.[9]

Halstead and Lind write boldly of the need to "reinvent" or "redesign" existing public and private structures, "not so much to shrink or expand government" as to "radically modernize it," "redesigning our nation's public, private, and communal institutions." "[W]e are interested not in tinkering at the margin... but rather in promoting, when necessary, a wholesale revamping of their component parts." The redesign will shift the "locus of decision-making" to individuals, "increasing the amount of choice," so as to "protect them from many of the uncertainties associated with relying on intermediary institutions."[10]

"The guiding principle of an Information Age social contract should be to link all benefits directly to individuals rather than to employers or to other intermediary institutions." Halstead and Lind would therefore elevate many concerns to the national level. They believe in "cooperative federalism," which is "pragmatic, flexible, and evolving over time," requiring state and local governments to "cede authority to federal jurisdictions in cases where the outcome is the expansion of individual freedoms and choices." Over time, this has led to the "increasing nationalization of American society" favored by early federalists like Alexander Hamilton and James Madison, whom Halstead and Lind cite with approval.[11]

Halstead and Lind would have a mandatory private health-care system for all Americans, a guaranteed safety net for the unemployed, and mandatory retirement savings for all, with public subsidies to "top off" the accounts of low-income workers. They propose a program of "universal capitalism" to make all future Americans "stakeholders" by granting every child at birth a one-time gift of $6,000. They call this a "twenty-first century equivalent" of the Homestead Act and the home-mortgage interest deduction.[12]

They would also eliminate the "antiquated patchwork of state sales taxes" and replace them with a national consumption tax with funds "rebated" to the states. This consumption tax would be used to equalize spending on public schools per pupil nationwide, "the next logical step in the evolution of American public education." The "biggest problem plaguing America's education system" is the "large inequities in per pupil funding across the country." Nationalizing public-school funding should be debated before school choice or national school standards. The danger of losing local control over schools is "easily exaggerated" if some form of choice is included. With equal funding per pupil, school choice, and other reforms, public schools will reduce demand for private schools, minimizing their balkanizing influence.[13]

Halstead and Lind do not explicitly blame private schools for social diversity, but they do write that the United States should "aspire to be a unified melting-pot nation instead of a polarized multicultural one." They therefore advocate an end to race-based civil rights (affirmative action, quotas and preferences, racial categorization) and a shift to "color-blind public policies and strong antidiscrimination laws," which they believe are "the best hope for integrating our remarkably diverse population into a dynamic yet cohesive whole." They also propose cutting back on immigration of low-skill workers, who are a threat to cohesion and a source of poverty.[14]

To grease the skids for such reforms, Halstead and Lind would streamline legislative procedures impeding the passage of new laws. They would scrap the filibuster in the Senate and make it easier to end Senate debates and discharge bills from committee, to minimize party influence and "maximize the chance that legislation will be debated and voted upon."[15] They would institute on-line voting and modify with the electoral college by apportioning electors according to the popular vote, as is done in Maine and Nebraska. They would also enact instant run-off voting to ensure that elected officials actually have the support of a popular majority.

But Halstead and Lind are not entirely trusting of popular majorities, and this is typical of Communitarians. While Progressives look to direct democracy to make known the sovereign will of the People, Communitarians worry that the people can't decide the many technical questions that modern governance faces. They therefore prefer representative democracy, trusting elected and appointed officials more than polls, plebiscites, and referenda to make the difficult decisions that common people are not qualified to make. "There is no single, coherent, enduring national majority; rather, there are multiple majorities," they write. "If the president—and the president alone—has a mystical 'mandate' from the American people, then disagreement with the president's policies must be rejection of the 'will of the people.'" The result would be an "electoral dictatorship."[16]

At the same time, Halstead and Lind prefer that their officials not be too bound by constitutional restraints. After all, they write, "The U.S. Constitution is an impressionistic sketch that can inspire a variety of broadly similar structures, not a blueprint specifying everything in advance." Halstead and Lind share Thomas Jefferson's disdain for legal traditionalism and quote him at length on the subject. They close *The Radical Center* claiming: "National reinvention is not a threat to the American tradition. It is the American tradition."[17]

The Radical Center is centrism inside the circle—practical, populist, and patriotic, if somewhat statist when viewed from above. Farther down, outside the circle, the Communitarians' concern for unity, community, and connectedness intensifies, along with their dissatisfaction with the failure of "intermediary institutions" and their aversion to the "narrow particularism" of ideology and self-interest. America is "bowling alone," writes Harvard's Robert Putnam, and that's not good:

Television, two-career families, suburban sprawl, generational changes in values—these and other changes in American society have meant that fewer and fewer of us find that the League of Women Voters, or the United Way, or the Shriners, or the monthly bridge club, or even a Sunday picnic with friends fits the way we have come to live. Our growing social-capital deficit threatens educational performance, safe neighborhoods, equitable tax collection, democratic responsiveness, everyday honesty, and even our health and happiness.[18]

"We need to connect with one another," Putnam told *The Washington Post* in 2001. "We've got to move a little more in the direction of community in the balance between community and the individual."[19]

But what to do about this growing "social-capital deficit"? The Communitarians cannot say that we should all join the Shriners or go bowling, much less get married and go to church. No, that would be divisive. They can only recommend community in general—and public programs to encourage it. Their interest in the various intermediary institutions of "civil society" is instrumental: they are valued for their contribution to society at large. Society at large is the Communitarians' ultimate interest, and the only way that society at large is defined is as the political community of the national state. The Communitarian approach is therefore necessarily national. Let others take up the cause of states, individuals, minorities, parents, churches, or chamber of commerce; the Communitarians' great cause is the nation.

This is the cause of the self-styled "communitarian movement" that arose in the late 1980s in reaction to the antigovernment individualism of the Reagan coalition and the antisocial individualism of civil libertarians and radical feminists. "Here lies the critical error of the age," declared Amitai Etzioni in 1984, "Maximization of individualism will serve neither the economy nor the community. Nor will it serve individual well-being."[20]

Etzioni runs the Communitarian Network, a loose association of community-minded academics, mostly centrist in orientation. The network has a quarterly journal, *The Responsive Community*, and a platform entitled "The Responsive Communitarian Platform: Rights and Responsibilities." The platform is intentionally vague so as to attract as many signatories as possible. It declares that communitarians are "not majoritarian, but strongly democratic." They are for "ordered liberty (rather than unlimited license)." They are against special interests, corruption, consumerism, particularism, and greed. They are for education, social justice, the environment, gun control, and the two-parent family. They are out "to rebuild America's moral foundation," not through coercion or censorship but through moral education. They are for truth-telling "generally." They are for dialogue, discussion, and experimentation. They are for strengthening civil society through partnerships with government. They are for national service, local service, and voluntarism. They look forward to the "emergence of a global community" and the "long-imagined community of humankind."

These Communitarians got a lot of early attention from Etzioni's attacks on the antisocial Left. Etzioni named the American Civil Liberties Union as "Public Enemy Number One." He declared a need for a "general shoring up of our moral foundations" against "moral confusion and social anarchy." He bemoaned the "anti-nuclear family mentality" that put self-actualization and "asocial gratification" ahead of raising children. He judged the two-parent family the best possible arrangement, arguing for a division of labor within the family: one parent to be supportive and protective, the other to push the child toward achievement. He denounced the deployment of military mothers during the Gulf War and once condemned day-care centers as "kennels for kids." "Quality time occurs within quantity time," he wrote in his 1993 book *The Spirit of Community*. "We have made a mistake in assuming that strangers can be entrusted with the effective personality formation of infants and toddlers. Over the past twenty-five years, we have seen the future, and it is not a wholesome one."[21]

Even so, Etzioni is no conservative. He sees Communitarians in a third position opposed to both conservative Christian "Authoritarians" and selfish individualistic "Libertarians." He writes that evangelist Jerry Falwell's Moral Majority "raised the right questions" but "provided the wrong, largely authoritarian and dogmatic answers." Other answers are needed to keep us out of the "dark tunnel of moralism and authoritarianism that leads to a church-dominated state or a right-wing world."[22]

After a decade, Communitarians are still searching for those answers. "We need a clearer vision of where the centrist way leads or in which direction we ought to pave it," Etzioni admits in his 2001 book *Next: The Road to the Good Society*. "We seek vision that inspires, compels, and gives meaning to our endeavors and sacrifices, to life."[23]

Etzioni's latest vision of the good society relies heavily on government. He would have a government-appointed "science court" decide how best to raise children. He wants a "massive increase" in spending for primary and secondary education. He wants "community jobs" for the unemployed and a "rich basic minimum standard of living, irrespective of their conduct," for food, shelter, clothing, and health care. He seeks a balance between the state and the market: "The United States may have overshot the point of balance, giving the market too much weight in recent years. The United Kingdom and Holland might be closer to the point of balance."[24]

Etzioni also looks to the various nonprofit, nonstate "communities" to do more, but he looks to government to get them going. He calls for the White House to order a "special review of all existing public policies and procedures that affect communities." He proposes a cabinet-level "Community Development Agency" to spur the expansion of nonprofit service groups. He writes that "the government needs to do more to foster communities where they exist and to prime their development where they have failed."[25]

In all his works, Etzioni has shown the Communitarian's concern for national unity. Americans need to "shore up the bonds that make America a nation." They need a "return to we-ness" and not a "retreat from nation." They "may now have to say that duty calls for having children" to avoid the "considerable negative consequences" of the "children deficit." They need to "relegitimate national policymaking." They need national service as an "antidote to the ego-centered mentality." They need a "limited extension of the existing category of punishable speech."[26] They need national education standards to promote consensus:

One of the reasons for the low consensus-building capacity of American society is that the schools are locally run. They do not subscribe to common national curriculum, and they transmit different sets of regional, racial, or class values. . . . As a result, young Americans grow up with relatively few shared values, symbols, or paradigms that many other communities draw upon to form consensus.[27]

At times, this call to national unity conflicts with the demands of diversity. On one hand, "unbounded pluralism" is "unwholesome." On the other hand, "Assimilation is unnecessarily homogenizing." Etzioni seeks "diversity within unity" for our national "community of communities." As a model, he suggests the kibbutz. "This vision of contained yet thriving communities is not without precedent," he writes. "Members of kibbutzim have strong conceptions of what is expected of members of their respective communities, but at the same time, no one is denied the right to free speech, assembly, and so on."[28]

Of course, a kibbutz is a commune with little or no ethnic or religious diversity, but as a Communitarian ideal, nothing else comes close.

Chapter 4

Change Is Good: The Progressive

All eyes are opened or opening to the rights of man. The general spread of the light of science has already laid open to every view the palpable truth, that the mass of mankind has not been born with saddles on their backs, nor a favored few, booted and spurred, ready to ride them legitimately by the grace of God.

Thomas Jefferson
Letter to the Mayor of Washington and the American People
June 24, 1826

The liberal imagination sits upon a triad of faith: an optimistic approach toward social problems, an orientation toward the future, and a belief in democracy.

David P. Barash
The L Word, 1992

In *The L Word*, a post-Reagan apology for modern American liberalism, David Barash of the University of Washington names optimism, democracy, and the future as liberalism's "secular trinity." The three are closely related. All are bound up in the modern myth of progress. A myth is not a falsehood; it is a story that expresses a believed truth. As commonly told today, the history of the modern West is a story of progress, according to which the present is better than the past and the future will be better than the present.[1]

Faith in progress is nowhere so strong as in the lower left, where we find Barash's liberals. Liberals believe in progress more than they believe in liberty, which is why liberty doesn't make the cut for their secular trinity.

They are not libertarians. They are pickier than libertarians about their liberties, and their choices are often colored by their faith in progress. They prefer new liberties to old liberties—abortion rights to gun ownership, sexual freedom to the freedom of association. The liberty they desire most is freedom from the past—from the old *archê* of Christian faith, fatherhood, and feudalism.

In Chapter 2 we identified the lower left with the democratic tradition, which was liberal in being anti-monarchical, anti-aristocratic, anti-clerical, and often anti-Christian, but not so liberal in its enthusiasm for social planning and the redistribution of wealth, or in its embrace of absolute popular sovereignty, which recognizes no limits on what the People may do. In the nineteenth century, the same tradition produced both socialism and communism, but also milder forms of liberalism whose main interest was progressive government. The ranks of such pro-government liberals even included some theorists we today call "classical liberals."

Take the arch-liberal John Stuart Mill (1806–1873). Mill defined freedom broadly as the absence of all restraint, "whether the means used be physical force in the form of legal penalties, or the moral coercion of public opinion." At the same time, he upheld the utilitarian standard in public policy, with its goal of "the greatest happiness of the greatest number." Mill found happiness not in tradition or religion, but in throwing both off. He was therefore quite keen on the freedom of speech and conscience, but not so respectful of property rights when they stood in the way of progress. He backed inheritance taxes, land redistribution, rent controls, labor laws to protect the common man from capitalism, and a wider role for government in providing public services such as education. In his later life, he inclined toward Britain's "New Liberalism," which broadened the government's warrant by redefining *liberty* to mean, in the words of Thomas Hill Green (1836–1882), the "positive power or capacity of doing or enjoying something worth doing or enjoying."

The term *liberal* took hold in America thanks to the pragmatist philosopher John Dewey (1859–1952). Dewey had used several words to describe his politics of social planning, among them *corporate*, *organic*, and *progressive*. But fascists described their own approach as *corporate* and *organic*, and *progressive* in Dewey's day belonged to reform-minded movements on both the Left and the Right. Dewey therefore settled on *liberal* to describe a political perspective denying the existence of all fixed truths and stressing society's freedom to experiment and innovate.[2]

The name *liberal* has been accepted ever since to describe the pro-government Left in America, but not without objection. Conservatives and libertarians both claim to be the true liberals, based on different definitions of liberty. This forces a difficult dispute over the various liberalisms: Is yours classical or modern, American or European, conservative or progressive? The liberals of the lower left are modern, American, and progressive. In fact, the more extreme among them prefer the name *progressive*, dismissing less extreme fellow travelers as "mere liberals." Some even dare to admit that their demands are hardly liberal in the classical sense, for they would include limits on speech and active efforts to eradicate errors of conscience. Others in the lower left use *liberal* and *progressive* interchangeably. We will do so also, but call them all Progressives.

In *The L Word*, David Barash defines liberalism as a happy mean between radicalism and conservatism. In the words of Supreme Court Justice Louis Brandeis, "Radicals, who would take us back to the roots of things, often fail because they disregard the fruit Time has produced and preserved. Conservatives fail because they would preserve even what Time has decomposed." Liberals, Barash writes, aim at "preserving that which is useful from the past, while adapting it to the present and future."[3]

In fact, the Progressive's regard for the past is not nearly so benign. In her 1996 book *It Takes a Village*, Hillary Clinton complains of "nostalgia merchants" hawking "Norman Rockwell-like" fantasies of days gone by:

There were many good things about our way of life back then. But in reality, our past was not so picture-perfect. Ask African-American children who grew up in a segregated society, or immigrants who struggled to survive in sweatshops and tenements, or women whose life choices were circumscribed and whose work was underpaid.[4]

Instead of building on the past as Barash suggests, Clinton is more inclined to turn her back on it:

We cannot move forward by looking to the past for easy solutions. Even if a golden age had existed, we could not simply graft it onto today's busier, more impersonal and complicated world. Instead, our challenge is to arrive at a consensus of values and a common vision of what we can do today, individually and collectively, to build strong families and communities.[5]

Barash himself allows that not everything old is bad, but promptly warns that "the past is also the fossilized consequences of long-ago abuses and neglect, and often it is a heavy weight that threatens to drag down the future."[6]

Radicals and Progressives differ greatly on this matter. Whereas Radicals are more pro-past and anti-present, Progressives are more pro-present and anti-past. Progressives see the problem as all those vestiges of a hated past that slow the march of progress. Radicals don't believe the myth of progress, for progress has only gotten us to the intolerable present. They work to overthrow the present so as to return to a simpler time in the long past.

Progressives believe in progress because they believe in their own goodness and in the perfectibility of the human race. Both notions come from the French Enlightenment. Barash quotes approvingly the Marquis de Condorcet (1743–1794): "No bounds have been fixed to the improvement of the human faculties . . . the perfectability of man is absolutely indefinite."[7] He also accepts Rousseau's insistence that since people are good deep down, evil must be a problem with the outside world. "To liberals," Barash writes, "evil is the result of a bad social order; people are fundamentally well-meaning (so long as they are secure, and thus unlikely to fall prey to unreason and resort to violence)."[8]

This externalization of evil is what leads Progressives to emphasize what Martin Luther King Jr. called "social sin," which contributes to the bad social order, as opposed to "individual sin," which is a strictly personal fault. Stealing is bad, but denying a man a job because of his race is worse because it enforces an unjust social order, which pushes people to steal. Progressives reject the Christian focus on individual sin, especially as it appears in the Roman Catholic doctrine of original sin and the Calvinist doctrine of natural depravity. Barash writes:

Traditionally, liberals and especially liberal psychotherapies have sought to help people overcome a sense of guilt in their private lives—about their "bad thoughts" or their secret, trivial, nasty deeds—while at the same time, paradoxically, encouraging a sense of guilt in their public lives. . . . Conservatives reverse the liberal priority, pounding home with evangelical zeal the idea of guilt in our private lives, while favoring blissful indifference to the sins of society.[9]

Barash even thinks the Christian view actually contributes to the bad social order, for "there is undeniably an abusive strain in an ideology so convinced of human imperfection that it justifies harshness and violence. . . and often generates harshness and violence in return." Others have argued that Christian patriarchy and traditional sexual mores produce "authoritarian personalities" prone to violence, tyranny, and fascism.[10]

The Progressive position on individual sin is moral relativism. Barash writes that "liberalism is in fact an ideology of relativism rather than absolutes." While conservatives believe in definite rights and wrongs, he writes, "Liberals are different. They believe in diversity, in the privatization of morality. They detest moral imperialism."[11]

Progressives often champion alternative lifestyles and disrespect social norms, which they see as socially constructed. Clinton insists throughout

It Takes a Village that there is no one right way to live: "There is no set formula for parenting success.... There is no magic formula for raising children ... there is no formula for how women should lead their lives." But there is a problem with teens having sex, and Clinton thinks that it might be because parents "are confused about their own values or the values they think are appropriate to teach to children."[12] No wonder.

But moral relativism only goes so far among Progressives, who in fact reserve their relativism for things like sex, sex roles, and religion. This is a problem that Barash admits but does not solve:

In their own defense, liberals sometimes argue that morality ought not be legislated. This is a slippery slope, however, ... the next step is a kind of moral relativism: "Who is to say what is right?" But if values aren't worth defending, then what about the values of tolerance, fairness, liberty, diversity, rationality, etc.?—that is, the basic tenets of liberalism itself. Clearly, there are decent, humane values that warrant being legislated and enforced.[13]

In fact, some Progressives are quite willing to impose their morality on others through centralized public education; laws against discrimination, harassment, and offensive speech; and an insistence on what Progressives themselves formerly called "political correctness," especially in the selection of people in power, like federal judges.

In contrast to anti-government Radicals, Progressives are fearlessly pro-government and brightly optimistic about the government's part in perfecting the social order. They affirm a positive role for government as an agent of improvement first and order second, reversing the conservative priority, which emphasizes keeping order and enforcing the law, based on a belief in human sinfulness. Believing instead that evil is ultimately external to the person, Progressives concentrate on eliminating external conditions that cause people to misbehave.

The external conditions seen as most likely to cause misbehavior are ignorance and inequality. Progressives are therefore big fans of education, especially public education, since private education is so prone to produce unequal results that perpetuate other inequalities. Inequality is bad because it creates resentment and desperation among the poor and powerless, who might then misbehave and threaten the public peace. "A two-tiered society will undermine the stability and moral authority of this nation," warns Robert Reich in his memoir of his years as Secretary of Labor under President Clinton.[14]

Reich's mention of "moral authority" hints at an even bigger reason why equality is so important to Progressives: Inequality destroys democracy, which Progressives define not as majority rule, but as whatever the People want. The *absolute sovereignty of popular desire* is central to the Progressives' denial of all other moral authorities. Inequality threatens that sovereignty by establishing an archy of some people and their values over other people and theirs. When this happens, the People lose their democratic liberty to satisfy themselves as they will. The limits of life become fixed by the powers that be and no longer subject to challenge. Democracy—as a societal system based on the denial of *archê*—ceases to exist.

As a rule, Progressives therefore favor policies that create equality. They may have given up on socialism and communism as the best path to equality, but they still worry that prosperity achieved through the free market will exacerbate inequalities that frustrate true democracy. Even if everyone prospers in a free market, some will prosper more than others, and those who prosper more will have more to say about what is right and what is wrong.

Progressives presume that more democracy will bring all the good things that they want to see. "If the political system actually worked for the majority," wrote the late Senator Paul Wellstone of Minnesota in his book *The Conscience of a Liberal*, "then certainly much more would already have been done for education, affordable child care, and health security for families. Congress would pass sweeping campaign finance reform as well."[15]

Wellstone spoke for both Progressives and Radicals when he warned that democracy is under threat from the "systemic corruption" of Big Money:

We do not have true democracy because our political system does not work for the people. Instead, well-paid corps of lobbyists and moneyed interests perpetuate the status quo. These power brokers rob the people of their ability to exercise authority, at least in free and open elections in which the best ideas and the best candidates prevail.[16]

For sincere Progressives, campaign finance reform is more than a ploy for power; it is a necessary reform to free democracy from what Bill Moyers has called the "legal bribe." Barash might look optimistically to the future, "in which democracy will be triumphant: not only political democracy, but economic and social democracy as well." But Wellstone worried that without reform, "The road leads to plutocracy. Not 'government of the people, by the people, and for the people' but government of the few, by the few, and for the few."[17]

The late twentieth century was not especially kind to Progressives. Ronald Reagan made *liberalism* a bad word. Two decades of prosperity sapped strength from the Democratic Party's usual base. The abject failure of the Soviet system seemed to settle the great debate between capitalism and communism. Even Progressives were forced to admit that free-marketers like Friedrich Hayek were right, at least about capitalism's wealth-creating potential.

Such events have sparked dissension in the lower left, as Democrats argue over which way to go. Some like Robert Reich are still holding fast to the old-time religion, but others, like Al From of the Democratic Leadership Council, think the time has come to revise the party's thinking a little, especially on economics. Progressives are caught in a tug-of-war between idealistic, socially minded Radicals and pragmatic, politically minded Communitarians.

The tension between them is evident in the person of Benjamin Barber, professor of civil society at the University of Maryland and an unofficial advisor to President Bill Clinton. Barber is a good example of today's conflicted Progressive. He is proud of his Radical roots and sympathies, but cognizant of the practical problem of winning and exercising power. His book *The Truth of Power* tells of his disappointment that practical politics left so little room for progressive reform in the Clinton White House, despite the president's personal interest and patronage.

Barber's radical credentials are beyond dispute. Besides his active role in the leadership of the Boston Committee for a Sane Nuclear Policy, he was a delegate for Eugene McCarthy when McCarthy ran as the Radical alternative to Robert F. Kennedy and Hubert Humphrey for the Democratic presidential nomination in 1968. Barber writes, "We were true radicals: critics of government, adversaries of centralized power, skeptics of the 'just wars' America was supposed to wage in the name of other peoples' rights, and cynics about universities in the clutches of highly ideologized professors."[18]

Even in his Clinton years, Barber considered himself an "old radical." He was a friend of the Democratic Leadership Council (DLC), but a friend on its left. He confesses persistent "doubts about the DLC approach" and worries that Will Marshall of the DLC's Progressive Policy Institute is trying to "charm capitalism into the Democratic fold." He admires Hillary Clinton's "ancient ardor of class war," speaks respectfully of Robert Reich's "redistributionist radicalism," and reserves his strongest censure for those on his right. When, at a White House dinner, Alan Ehrenhalt laments the loss of respect for authority, Barber is appalled. "Authority?" he writes. "For antiwar baby boomers who remember sixties slogans like 'Resist illegitimate authority,' an appeal to authority was bound to arouse more hostility than sympathy." To Barber, Ehrenhalt's remarks "made clear why liberals worry about communitarians."[19]

But Barber is far too much an admitted "fan of government" to fit among today's Radicals. He imagines himself as a Voltaire whispering in the ear of his enlightened despot. He complains that Americans have become too paranoid of government, thanks in part to Hollywood conspiracy dramas like Oliver Stone's *Nixon* and *JFK*. He warns that both parties have made such use of the rhetoric of privatization and voluntarism that "warning bells no longer ring" when the public good comes under assault. He fears that, by declaring the "end of the era of big government," Clinton "reinforced the libertarian prejudices against government for which Americans already had rather too much sympathy."[20]

Much of his advice to Clinton was aimed at getting Americans more involved in politics and government. The problem, as Barber sees it, is James Madison's "quasi-aristocratic innovation of representation," which gave the United States a "nominally democratic constitution" that left most people with little or no role in government.[21] Barber advocates "participatory democracy," à la the Swiss system of "direct participation in governance through referenda and initiatives."

Democracy for Barber means everyone having his or her say in public. He trusts the masses to find their way through *isêgoria*, the ancient Greek right to speak at public assemblies: "For in the end human freedom will be found not in caverns of private solitude but in the noisy assemblies where women and men meet daily as citizens and discover in each other's talk the consolation and strength of their common humanity."[22]

Barber also advocates a system of national civilian service as a means of instilling civic-mindedness, another idea inspired by the Swiss and outlined in his 1984 book *Strong Democracy*. He contrasts the Old Democrat focus on what government can do for you with the New Democrat focus on what you can do for government. He also distinguishes the progressive focus on civic responsibility and civil society from the conservative focus on individual responsibility and voluntarism:

Conservatives often saw voluntarism as replacing a government that "doesn't work" rather than as a road to better government. Voluntary activity, "private" and largely apolitical, would entail a beneficent transfer of responsibility from public officials and democratic institutions to the private sector, where charity and philanthropy could take up the slack.

For progressives, however, voluntary service activity represented a strengthening of democracy, a devolution of power not to individuals and private corporations but to local democratic institutions and self-governing communities. It was a way to share responsibility and build partnerships between citizens and their elected officials, a way to pull down rather than put up walls between government and the rest of us.[23]

In other words, he writes, "Republicans wanted civil society to replace government; Democrats wanted it to reanimate citizenship and hence relegitimize government."[24]

At times Barber sounds downright communitarian with all his talk of civil society, but his leftist ideology keeps him out of that camp. When, at another White House dinner, his communitarian colleague William Galston bemoans the collapse of the traditional family and the resulting harm to society, Barber reminds him there and then that

... nostalgia for this world that never was had been a neocon excuse for refusing to confront the reality of social, religious, and political change in an ever more diversified society. The traditional family offered the consolation of solidarity and a sense of place but at the price of structural inequality and the disempowerment of women. Nor was there any way "back" to such a world, even were it desirable.[25]

Barber tells the gathering that America needs a "new story of the family" marked by "tolerance for diversity, by a willingness to accept pluralism" in the "new, multicultural America." In his book, he describes America as a "permanently racist nation." He praises the "open society" of Karl Popper and George Soros. He delights in the overthrow of "all-white, all-Anglo-Saxon, all-male America" by the Civil Rights Movement and the 1965 immigration reforms: "America has always been more multicultural and heterogeneous than its Protestant curators wished, but with the opening of the floodgates in 1965, the country was set to become the first truly global society."[26]

Progressives are the biggest fans of tolerance, inclusion, diversity, and multiculturalism, but deep in the lower left they are also openly hostile to cultures and values they don't like and quite willing to the use the force of law against such. Michael Walzer of *Dissent* magazine and Princeton's Institute for Advanced Study is a multiculturalist and a "social democrat" who strives for balance between the extremes of selfish individualism and oppressive community. He would use the power of the state to correct both, but his harshest words are aimed at religious traditionalists who teach doctrines that are "profoundly hostile to democratic politics":

Very strong ethnic national and religious communities are often oppressive to many of their members, most importantly to women. To be committed to a democratic society of which these women are supposedly equal citizens, you have to find some way to break into these communities and reshape their internal life. The only agent for doing that is the state and that means you need a strong sense of citizenship and common values in order to foster resistance or intervention in the groups.[27]

A favorite way "to break into these communities and reshape their internal life" is compulsory public education. After all, if people are naturally good, then evil must be learned, and if it is learned, then it can be unlearned. Progressives therefore work to "eradicate" evil through "reeducation." This indeed was the aim of the *Studies in Prejudice* series, funded fifty years ago by the American Jewish Committee, which produced *The Authoritarian Personality*. In the foreword to that work, the editors of the series write, "our aim is not merely to describe prejudice but to explain it in order to help in its eradication. Eradication means reeducation scientifically planned on the basis of understanding scientifically arrived at."[28]

Inside the circle, the moderate, populist, run-of-the-mill Progressive wants just what the Democratic Party promises: "active, effective government that focuses its efforts on people who truly need help," in the words of party Chairman Terry McAuliffe.[29] But what about well outside the circle, in the farthest reaches of the lower-left corner? Hillary Clinton gave us her view in her first major speech on health care back in April 1993:

We need a new politics of meaning. We need a new ethos of individual responsibility and caring. We need a new definition of civil society which answers the unanswerable questions posed by both the market forces and the governmental ones, as to how we can have a society that fills us up again and makes us feel that we are part of something bigger than ourselves.[30]

Clinton borrowed this "politics of meaning" from Michael Lerner, rabbi, psychologist, editor and publisher of *Tikkun* magazine. Whatever Clinton meant by the phrase, her use of it raised a storm among her critics, and she soon stopped using it.

But Lerner himself later expanded on the theme in his 1996 book *The Politics of Meaning*. In the book, Lerner tells us that what America really needs is a new religion. "Most Americans hunger for meaning and purpose in life," he writes. "Yet we are caught within a web of cynicism that makes us question whether there could be any higher purpose besides material self-interest and looking out for number one."[31]

Lerner's desire is to "create a society that encourages and supports love and intimacy, friendship and community, ethical sensibility and spiritual awareness among people." By "spiritual awareness," he means "an awareness of the fundamental unity of all being and of our connectedness to one another and to the universe." Lerner wants to "change the bottom line," so that programs and institutions "foster ethically, spiritually, ecologically, and psychologically sensitive human beings who can maintain long-term, loving personal and social relationships." Lerner eschews the "patriarchal separation of work and caring" and the individualistic focus on contract and exchange. Instead, he says, we need an "economy of caring" based on "noncontractual realities of the mother-child relationship," informed by a feminist understanding of the "centrality of caring and nurturing relationships." His model society is Amitai Etzioni's, the Israeli kibbutz. Lerner writes:

As the Israeli kibbutz experience shows, even the most boring work can be fulfilling to workers when it is experienced as part of a larger project that has a transcendent meaning and is democratically shaped. When I worked on a kibbutz, I used to marvel at the degree to which garbage collectors, manure shovelers, chicken pluckers, and machinists in the kibbutz factory all could revel in their work, because in it they saw an expression of their contribution to the kibbutz or to the building of Zionism.[32]

Lerner lists three elements of the kibbutz experience that he thinks "relevant to building a sense of community in the American workplace: seeing work as relevant to the common good, governing work democratically, and having the possibility of job rotation and Sabbatical years."[33] Toward that ideal, Lerner calls for an expanded national service program, with everyone required to perform five hours of community service per week. He wants "democratic mechanisms to balance the market" and imagines workers committees taking a few days once a year to develop "mission statements" and evaluate their organization's performance. He reminds his readers that he has not called for redistributing wealth or socializing ownership of corporations, but he reserves the right to do so later. "On this question," he writes, "I remain agnostic." If capitalism can foster the good feelings he thinks important, then it is a "viable economic form":

But if private ownership of the means of production becomes too great an obstacle, if capitalists band together to use their power to prevent democratization of the workplace and transformation of production toward the goal of serving the common good, then perhaps another form of ownership will be necessary.[34]

Chapter 5

Question Authority: The Radical

Government, like dress, is the badge of lost innocence; the palaces of kings are built on the ruins of the bowers of paradise.

Thomas Paine
Common Sense, 1776

Daddy, won't you take me back to Muhlenberg County, Down by the Green River where paradise lay? Well, I'm sorry, my son, but you're too late in askin'; Mr. Peabody's coal train has hauled it away.

John Prine "Paradise," 1971

Start at the center of our Compass and move left. The first position you pass is the populism of the late Eugene McCarthy, former senator from Minnesota. McCarthy was a pragmatic idealist with a strongly communal outlook and an independent mind. His sense of social justice was born of his Irish Catholic compassion for the poor and powerless. He was pro-farmer, pro-worker, anti-war, and anti-Washington. He distrusted both Big Business and Big Government, but often looked to the latter to look out for the little guy—struggling families, rural communities, racial minorities.

There aren't many like Eugene McCarthy left. He was too progressive for the Democratic Party in 1968, losing the presidential nomination to Hubert Humphrey. But he was already too conservative for the Democratic Party in 1972, when the nomination went to George McGovern.

Today the same shoes might be filled by author Norman Mailer, a self-described "Left-Conservative," perhaps even (he says in jest) a "left-medievalist." He is not happy with the modern world. He fears technology, the global economy, stratospheric disparities of wealth and power, and the allure of empire. He first entered politics as a candidate for mayor of New York in 1969. With columnist Jimmy Breslin as his running mate, Mailer headed a Left-Right anti-establishment coalition whose quasi-libertarian platform won the praise of anarcho-capitalist Murray Rothbard. Among other anti-government planks, Mailer called for the city's secession from the state and for a radical devolvement of power to the city's many neighborhoods.

The Mailer of today believes in both God and the devil. "So, I can hardly be a liberal," he told *The American Conservative*. "God is bad enough for them, but talk about the devil and the liberal's mind is blown. . . . That is the end of real conversation." He distinguishes between "value conservatives" (good) and "flag conservatives" (bad). Of the latter, he says:

What they really want is power. . . . They believe this country is the only hope of the world and they feel that this country is becoming more and more powerful on the one hand, but on the other hand, is rapidly growing more dissolute. And so the only solution for it is empire, World Empire.

He also worries about the effects of television on young minds, but most of all he worries about towering wealth. "Our first problem is not immigration, but the American corporation," he says. "That is the force which has succeeded in taking America away from us."[1]

The further left we move from the populist center, the less we hear about God and the more we hear about the corporate devil. Just to Mailer's left is former California governor and Oakland mayor Jerry Brown, another left-of-center populist with a somewhat religious outlook. A few more steps left we find the hardly religious Jim Hightower of Texas, author of *If the Gods Had Meant Us to Vote They Would Have Given Us Candidates* and *There's Nothing in the Middle of the Road But Yellow Stripes and Dead Armadillos*. Hightower has spent his life "battling the Powers That Be on behalf of the Powers That Ought To Be—consumers, working families, environmentalists, small businesses, and just-plain-folks." His political spectrum runs "not right to left but top to bottom."[2] In other words, what he's really against is not the coercion of political order, but the archy of the social order.

Still further left, out of the populist center, stretches a long line of radicals, left-libertarians, anti-authoritarians, socialists, anarchists, and environmental primitivists. Many along this line despise the name "liberal," which they apply disparagingly to the pro-government, establishment Left. Some call themselves "progressive," which fits a folk passionately opposed to the present and desperate for something different in the future. But these progressives are not all that fond of progress. In fact, progress is quite often a dirty word among them. It's the greedy grab of globalization. It's the capitalist cancer of urban sprawl. It's the noose tightening around the neck of the powerless poor. It's the coal train hauling away the old home-place in John Prine's song:

> Then the coal company came with the world's largest shovel,
> And they tortured the timber and stripped all the land.
> Well, they dug for their coal till the land was forsaken,
> And they wrote it all down as the progress of man.

The kind of progress these progressives want is a return to nature—to the free, equal, and fraternal state of nature into which human beings were first born, before pride and greed despoiled the earth and enslaved the people. "Man is born free, and everywhere he is in chains," Rousseau wrote. Like Rousseau, these progressives are both bitterly cynical and sublimely sentimental at the same time. They believe that the root of the problem is a corrupt civilization founded upon oppressive power structures. The only solution is to strike at the root and destroy or dismantle the structures. Thus they are often called *radicals* (from *radix*, Latin for root). They often call themselves radicals, so we will, too.

Radicals are always on the side of the subjects of power: small-time farmers, workers, women, children, people of color, gays, Native Americans, immigrants, convicted criminals, the poor, the oppressed, the disabled, the disenfranchised, the disadvantaged, the old, the odd, the obese—out-groups of most but not all kinds. They can be counted on to take the side of blacks under whites, Africans under Europeans, Latinos under Anglos, women under Muslims, Palestinians under Israelis, Serbs under NATO, Marxists under fascists, Buddhists under Beijing, and anybody under Americans. They cannot be counted on to support the underdog in the reverse of all these power relations. But in general, Radicals are for the people against the power. Their complaint is against subordination per se and the superstitions and inequalities that make it possible.

In times past, Radicals focused more on the old sources of archy—the feudal ranking of Medieval Europe, the Divine Right of Kings, the justification of patriarchy inherent in Christian theology, and age-old beliefs about men and women. All these have been overthrown, but the evil of economic inequality is worse than ever. The poor are still with us, and the rich are only getting richer. This is bad not because some people are still poor, but because other people are so much more powerful. The result is not merely material inequality, which in itself is not bad even to Radicals; the result is the ultimate injustice of subordination, the domination of some by others.

The Right often rests its defense of inequality on the wealth-creating capability of capitalism. This misses the point with Radicals. Progressives might still need to be convinced that capitalism creates wealth; Radicals do not. They see all too well that capitalism—whether corporatist or laissez-faire—makes some people very wealthy. But Radicals do not want wealth; they want justice, which capitalism threatens. For even when it makes everyone better off, it rewards some much more than others, perpetuating an archical society in which power is unevenly distributed.

Progressive attempts at *noblesse oblige* tied to the capital-friendly conditions of the "Third Way" only strengthen the archy by making the poor more dependent upon the power. That's why some Radicals revolted when the Democratic Party picked Al Gore and Joe Lieberman to run for president and vice president in 2000. Gore and Lieberman were both "New Democrats" associated with the Democratic Leadership Council (DLC). The DLC was the springboard of Bill Clinton, whom Radicals hated for his various betrayals: his "don't ask/don't tell" policy on gays in the military, his support for NAFTA and GATT, his reform of welfare, his expansion of NATO, his attacks on Sudan, Afghanistan, Iraq, and Serbia. "Impeach President Clinton," one Radical Web site demanded, "But For the Right Reasons."

Gore/Lieberman promised more of the same, which meant to Radicals that things would only get worse. "Frightened liberals are letting things get worse and worse for fear of doing anything," Green Party presidential candidate Ralph Nader told Ruth Conniff, Washington editor of *The Progressive*. "They keep letting the Republicans burglarize the country on behalf of corporations. And they raise money from the same corporations."[3]

The Green Party promised a government "of, by, and for the People . . . not monied interests." Its platform called for universal health care, affordable housing, public transit, stronger consumer-protection laws, easier access to courts in liability cases, the "living wage," the elimination of poverty, campaign finance reform, public funding of elections, and an end to "corporate welfare" (tax breaks, subsidies, free technology transfers, free use of government property, government funding of research, and unnecessary defense spending).

Many Democrats were pushing the same things, but most stuck with their party. Congressman Barney Frank of Massachusetts told Conniff of *The Progressive* that it was only a difference over strategy, not substance:

The purpose of voting is not catharsis. The purpose of voting is to help poor kids and gay kids who are getting beat up. It is to affect public policy. It's not to feel good emotionally. We share this country with 250 million other people. That means you almost never reach a consensus on everything. You have to ask, "What is most likely to move forward a social justice agenda?"[4]

But, as Frank's own words reveal, this is not just a difference over strategy, but over deeply seated sentiments. Politically minded Progressives like Frank are really most concerned about who wins and who loses, and who wields the power of government. They are thus less bothered by the necessary compromises and more content with their governmental gains for the progressive cause. They therefore do not share the anti-government alienation felt by many Radicals, whose thinking on these matters is more idealistic and less pragmatic. Contrasting Radicals and Progressives, Dwight Macdonald wrote, "The Progressive thinks in collective terms (the interests of society or of the working class); the Radical stresses individual conscience. . . . (He) is pleased if history is also going his way, but . . . stubborn about following his own road, that of 'ought' rather than 'is.' "[5]

The problem is that there just isn't any substitute for justice, so compromise can't possibly come easy for Radicals. Most others around the Compass are careful to avoid appearing too extreme, lest they be pushed beyond the pale of respectability. Progressives, Communitarians, and Neoconservatives are especially cautious in their concern to hold on to the center and so remain in power. But a burning passion for justice moves Radicals to pursue their principles to their logical extremes. This accounts for the furious diversity of thought and action among them, but also for their pervasive pessimism. "The law is not on our side, it just isn't," writes William Greider in his 1992 book *Who Will Tell the People: The Betrayal of American Democracy*. " 'Organized money' is ascendant and 'organized people' are inert because money has learned how to do modern politics more effectively than anyone else. . . . Money is power in American politics. It always has been."[6]

The realization that it always has been leaves Radicals in a love-hate relationship with politics and government. They have long sought to use government to protect the people from the monied interests, but their constant fear is that government has instead become a capitalist tool. Lately the latter has seemed more likely. The past, it seems, held higher hopes. "In my view," Noam Chomsky wrote in 1998, "the last liberal president was Richard Nixon. Since him, they've been nothing but conservatives (or what are called 'conservatives')." Alexander Cockburn and Ken Silverstein expressed much the same sentiment in 1996, calling the Nixon era an "age of enlightenment and promise." Nader himself now marvels that Nixon has become a "favorable standard of comparison" for today's Democrats. After all, he notes, Nixon gave us the Consumer Product Safety Commission, the Occupational Safety and Health Agency, the Environmental Protection Agency, wage and price controls, and the all-volunteer military.[7]

Since Nixon, there has only been retrenchment. The culture wars may have gone the Radicals' way. The world has been made safe for gay capitalists like Andrew Sullivan. But corporate power is stronger than ever, and government is ever more on its side. This has inspired deep soul-searching among many Radicals.

Barbara Ehrenreich thought the federal government was headed in the right direction before Reagan, toward "our goal of an economically socialist and socially libertarian society." But by 1996, after two decades of "conservative national governance, Reagan through Clinton," she is convinced something has gone wrong. She wrote about it in *The Nation*, under the subtitle "Confessions of a Recovering Statist":

The federal government of 1997 is a very different creature from that of, say, 1977—more egregiously corrupt and sycophantic toward wealth, more glaringly repressive and even less responsive to the needs of low- and middle-income people. . . . While government does less and less for us, it does more and more *to* us. The right points to the appalling firebombing at Waco; we should be just as noisily indignant about the ongoing police war against low-income Americans of color, not to mention teenagers, immigrants and other designated misfits. If there is a handy measure of a government's repressiveness, it is the proportion of its citizenry who are incarcerated, and at least by this measure the United States leads the world.[8]

Ehrenreich complains that the feds now tax the poor to pay for corporate welfare and the military, and even programs for the poor are "tainted by the repressive agenda of the right, which has budgeted funds for 'chastity education' for welfare recipients" and backed "intimate monitoring of the lifestyles" of public-housing tenants. The solution, she says, is more *nongovernmental* action, like union organizing, civil-rights litigation, and a variety of protests and public-service projects that progressives can undertake on their own: "If government won't do it, then let government get out of the way, because we're not waiting around!"

Radicals have long relied on the "democratic" social organizations of civil society—unions, civic groups, nonprofits, and other nongovernmental organizations (NGOs)—to counter the power of archical social organizations like families, churches, and corporations. In recent years, NGOs also have been extra active in helping to overthrow and replace repressive regimes overseas. Throughout Eastern Europe, Western powers have relied on NGOs like George Soros's Open Society Fund to award aid, direct political development, monitor human rights, and, especially, provide ideological intelligence—pointing out the good guys and the bad guys, from a leftist perspective.

Lately, however, Radicals have begun to worry that the NGOs of civil society have grown too close to the power. David Rieff writes in *The Nation* that the advocates of civil society have become "useful idiots of global-ization," advancing the "dominant ideology of the post-cold war period: liberal market capitalism." Rieff sees reliance on civil society by Bill Clinton's and Tony Blair's "Third Way" as part of a broader corporatist scheme to privatize the world. In this sense, privatization does not mean freedom from government, but integration into the global corporate system, in which both governments and NGOs are merely parts of the machine. Rieff warns that NGOs are not democratic organizations. They operate beyond public scrutiny, their leaders are unelected, their books are never audited, they are accountable to no one. Yet, he writes, these "unaccountable, un-democratic congeries of single-interest groups" are being proposed as the "only viable alternative to the nation-state." They thus threaten the world with a "new medievalism, with the leaders of the NGOs as feudal lords."[9]

Here we have another difference between Radicals and Progressives. Progressives have been the boldest about declaring the end of the nation-state and the emergence of the global nation. They have been the biggest fans of global government through international bureaucracies like NATO, the United Nations, the European Union, the World Trade Organization, the World Bank, the World Court, the International Criminal Court, the International Monetary Fund, and the growing array of international conventions superseding old-fashioned, inefficient, ethnocentric national sovereignty. Radicals, by contrast, view all of these new bureaucracies with suspicion and distrust. They would often use them for the same purposes as Progressives, to defend the environment, workers, and women. But they are far more fearful that these bureaucracies, once established, will become merely more coercive parts of the corporate machine, working to globalize, privatize, commercialize, and homogenize the world, for the fun and profit of the few.

Radicals are therefore opposed not just to Big Business but to Big Government. The Green Party, in fact, lists "decentralization" as the fifth of its "Ten Key Values":

Centralization of wealth and power contributes to social and economic injus-tice, environmental destruction, and militarization. Therefore, we support a re-structuring of social, political, and economic institutions away from a system that is controlled by and mostly benefits the powerful few, to a democratic, less bureaucratic system. Decision making should, as much as possible, remain at the individual and local level, while assuring that civil rights are protected for all citizens.[10]

The other nine key values are, in order: grassroots democracy, ecological wisdom, social justice and equal opportunity, nonviolence, community-based economics, feminism, respect for diversity, personal and global responsibility, and "future focus and sustainability."

No survey of modern Radicals could leave out Noam Chomsky. A prolific writer, Chomsky holds the record for the most titles in stock on politics at the bookstore across the street from the National Press Building in Washington, D.C. The store has twenty-two titles by Chomsky, more than twice as many as the runner-up, Karl Marx.

Chomsky describes himself as an anarchist and a "libertarian socialist." Both terms make sense according to our Compass. A libertarian socialist would be midway between the libertarian Individualists of the upper left and the socialist Progressives of the lower left. An anarchist would be found at the far left of the A scale, the scale of *archê*. (Recall that Ehrenreich describes her own views as "economically socialist and socially libertarian." Chomsky and Ehrenreich were both members of Nader's 2000 campaign committee, the Citizens' Committee for Nader-LaDuke. Jim Hightower was a co-chair.)[11]

In all his words and works, Chomsky sounds many standard Radical themes. Sports engender "jingoist and chauvinist attitudes." Team sports "build up irrational attitudes of submission to authority." Corporations are "private despotisms." No society dominated by them can be free. "What kind of freedom is there inside a corporation? They're totalitarian institutions—you take orders from above and maybe give them to people below you. There's about as much freedom as under Stalinism."[12]

Chomsky believes the American constitutional system is rigged against democracy. James Madison was most concerned to protect the interests of rich landowners like himself, "so he designed a system that made sure democracy couldn't function." Alexander Hamilton turned the United States into a capitalist state, but the United States is not now a capitalist state because big business is too close to government; a capitalist state would require laissez faire. Franklin Delano Roosevelt, in typical Progressive fashion, "left power in the hands of the rich, but bound them to a kind of social contract."[13]

That's not good enough for Chomsky: "I don't think we should live in a society where the rich and powerful determine how public money is spent." Democracy must therefore be "fully participatory," ensuring relative equality of property and prosperity for all. "Any true democracy has to be what we call today a welfare state—actually, an extreme form of one, far beyond anything envisioned in this century." In a "genuinely democratic society," even the media would be "under public control." And, of course, the corporations have got to go:

Corporations are fundamentally illegitimate, and they don't have to exist at all in their modern form. . . . Just as other oppressive institutions—slavery, say, or royalty—have been changed or eliminated, so corporate power can be changed or eliminated. What are the limits? There aren't any. Everything is ultimately under public control.[14]

Chomsky bases his hopes on a very Rousseauian trust in a sense of justice embedded in human nature, in contrast to the more modern, materialistic, pragmatic view, which attributes our sense of justice to the external forces of socialization. Chomsky tells Alexander Cockburn:

. . . there must be principles that are embedded in our nature or at the core of our understanding of what a decent human life is, what a proper form of society is and so on . . . the idea that human beings are malleable and that people don't have an instinctive nature is a very attractive one to people who want to rule, and to control.[15]

The notion of an innate sense of justice is also found in Christian teaching, but whereas Christians usually assume that natural justice requires archy, Chomsky assumes that natural justice requires anarchy: People don't need anyone over them telling them what is right because they already know it.

As for the "managerial intelligentsia" who prefer the malleable view of human nature, Chomsky says they turn up on both the Left and the Right, as either Leninists or capitalists:

Leninism is the ideology of a radical intelligentsia that says "we have a right to rule." Alternatively, they have joined the decision-making sector of state capitalist society as managers in the political economic and ideological institutions. The ideologies are very similar. . . . All of this was predicted by the anarchist Bakunin, probably the only prediction in the social sciences that's ever come true.[16]

The abuses of the Leninist Left are increasingly the concern of Alexander Cockburn, longtime columnist for *The Nation*, now also editor of *CounterPunch*. Born and raised in Ireland, Cockburn comes by his radicalism honestly: His father, Claud Cockburn, was a leading voice in Britain's Communist Party in the 1930s and 1940s. Cockburn admits to being a leftist and a "radical," but resists other labeling. Others on the Left are wont to describe him (like Chomsky) as a "libertarian socialist." His journal *CounterPunch* boasts, "Ours is muckraking with a radical attitude . . . we have many friends and all the right enemies."[17]

The central theme throughout all of Cockburn's work is a deep distrust of the forces of order, social and political. He deplores the use of drugs like Prozac and Ritalin for social control. He takes sides with the Branch Davidians at Waco and the Church of Scientology in Germany, against the Cult Awareness Network and the government agencies that persecute such dissenters. He doubts the authenticity of prehistoric cave paintings in France and suspects they might be part of a government program to encourage culture. He assumes at the start that government is at least a potential enemy, writing in *Washington Babylon*, with Ken Silverstein, that "for an independent citizenry the correct, and indeed democratic, approach is not to trust 'government'—not in ancient Greece, and not in America today."[18]

That goes for all governments, even those headed by such Progressive heroes as John F. Kennedy, Jimmy Carter, and Bill Clinton. Cockburn panned Oliver Stone's *JFK* for its pious portrayal of the man responsible for the Bay of Pigs and Operation Mongoose (an attempt to assassinate Cuba's Fidel Castro). He faults Carter for creating Nicaragua's *contras* and Afghanistan's *mujahideen*. He blames Clinton for the incincration of the Branch Davidians, the deaths of Iraqi children under economic sanctions, and the 1999 bombing of Yugoslavia, ridiculing the last as the "First Progressives' War." Of Clinton's impeachment, Cockburn wrote, "What the stuffy left forgets is that sex scandals can be an important component of the seditious ridiculing of Established Power, one of the prime tasks of any leftist worth the name . . . any good leftist should want impeachment to be a staple of every president."

Cockburn has often annoyed *The Nation*'s readers with his digs at the Leninists of the lower left—gays who would censor Dr. Laura, feminists who stood by Clinton. A few years back, Cockburn had readers hyperventilating over his visit to a gun show in Detroit called "Gunstock." He found the attendees "amiable characters" and suggested to his readers that they start handing out copies of *The Nation* at gun shows, to open a dialogue with sympathetic anti-establishment types. "There was an absolute torrent of outrage," he wrote later of his readers' response. "People didn't think that was a good idea at all."[19]

Even worse, in 2000 Cockburn accepted an invitation to speak at a conference sponsored by Justin Raimondo's Antiwar.com, knowing full well that the other speakers would include Patrick J. Buchanan. How could he, a horrified fan wanted to know, when Buchanan's policies "could only be called fascist"? Cockburn replied:

I don't mind sharing a conference schedule with someone who opposes war on Serbs and on Iraqi kids. Nor do I think B[uchanan] is any more of a fascist—in practical terms—than Albright and Clinton and Gore and Bradley, with the first three literally with the blood of millions on their hands.[20]

Not long ago, Michael Albert, co-founder and co-editor of *Z Magazine*, provided a succinct summation of the extreme Radical perspective in the following definition of anarchism:

Most broadly an anarchist seeks out and identifies structures of authority, hierarchy, and domination throughout life, and tries to challenge them as conditions and the pursuit of justice permit. Anarchists work to eliminate subordination. They focus on political power, economic power, power relations among men and women, power between parents and children, power among cultural communities, power over future generations via effects on the environment, and much else as well. Of course anarchists challenge the state and the corporate rulers of the domestic and international economy, but they also challenge every other instance and manifestation of illegitimate authority.[21]

This might sound extreme, but Albert was actually writing against a trend in anarchism that he found even more extreme, a trend responsible for embarrassingly violent protests by young devotees of a "not so desirable anarchism." In a follow-up article, Albert cited as the best exemplar of this other anarchism, the anti-civilizational primitivism of John Zerzan.

John Zerzan beats Jean-Jacques Rousseau at his own game. Zerzan rejects all of the hallmarks of human civilization: language, mathematics, division of labor, specialization, and, of course, technology. His "working hypothesis" is that division of labor separates the good old days from the hard times that followed. "Specialization divides and narrows the individual, brings in hierarchy, creates dependency and works against autonomy.... tools or roles that involve division of labor engender divided people and divided society." Geometry was invented "to measure fields for purposes of ownership, taxation, and the assignment of slave labor." Numbers themselves depersonalize life. "When members of a large family sit down to dinner, they know immediately, without counting, whether someone is missing. Counting becomes necessary only when things become homogenized." Even language is a "means of oppression." Language "conceals and justifies, compelling us to suspend our doubts about its claim to validity. It is at the root of civilization, the dynamic code of civilization's alienated nature."[22]

In his critique of Zerzan, Albert argued that technology per se is neutral and could be used for good or ill; that division of labor is necessary and good, as long as it does not "relegate many to obedience and rote boredom while privileging an elite few with empowering and engaging endeavors"; that all societies "need to fulfill adjudicative, legislative, and implementation functions," and therefore political structures, institutions, and reforms can be used legitimately to advance anarchist ends; that primitivism, *reductio ad absurdum*, would mean the elimination of sex, consciousness, and the human race; and that "good anarchism" is primarily social and only secondarily political, and therefore it is appropriately focused not on destroying the state or the civilization, but on building better, anarchical (i.e., non-archical) ways of life.

Albert's arguments stirred up an e-maelstrom among anarchists. The devotees of "not so desirable anarchism" were incensed and incredulous. Albert is not an anarchist, they insisted. He's a liberal! He's a leftist! He's a Leninist! He's a social democrat! He's an authoritarian! "Like all authoritarians, he urges unity and collaboration, but only on his terms, never on ours." "Like all (aspiring) leaders, Albert is very concerned about the legitimacy of his own authority." "Like all leftists, his project is to appoint/elect/mandate better, wiser rulers. Anarchists want no rulers; that is why we are anarchists."[23]

Most of the debate revolved around the issue of authority: what it was and what made it legitimate. Some critics would only accept authority that was entirely voluntary, temporary, and informal. One wrote, "it's not authority 'per se' to which I object; if I want to learn a skill, I naturally find a skilled person to share her/his knowledge with me." Most objected to "institutionalized" authority: "This arises when someone with that skill uses their knowledge of it as a way to sustain and perpetuate power differentials with her/his peers." Many would not accept authority as legitimate if it involved any kind of control: "Anarchists believe that any control is inappropriate and illegitimate; that is why we are anarchists."[24]

Albert responded patiently, courteously, and indefatigably through 87 pages of outrage and insults. He argued that authority could be consensual and therefore legitimate; they accused him of being a democrat and a majoritarian. He argued that society needed some way to "adjudicate" and "legislate," so as to maintain "norms"; they rejected these as "statist assumptions." He argued that parents, at the very least, must have some limited authority over children. To argue otherwise, he said, would mean that "a child's will should prevail over an adult's, by definition, in every circumstance." But even this was too much. "As for the child's will 'prevailing,' that just shows how stuck he is in authoritarian thinking. Must all relationships have one person who prevails and one who is therefore vanquished? Besides, in a battle of wills, adults usually exercise power over children rather than authority."[25] (Here, of course, *power* means *kratos* and *authority* means *archê*.)

Albert obviously wasn't anarchical enough for these anarchists, who inhabit the outer limits of our Compass, at the furthest leftward extent of the A scale. Here, anarchists strive to construct functioning organizations without "institutional authority" (as they define it, the ranking of some people over others—in a word, *archy*). "Just remember one thing. We have no leaders," says the Web site of the Mobilization of Global Justice (MGJ), which organizes the protests Albert thinks are undesirable.[26]

Instead of leaders to make decisions and give direction, MGJ operates by "consensus decision making." Consensus does not mean that everyone agrees with the decision taken. It means that "no one felt that her/his position on the matter was misunderstood or that it wasn't given a proper hearing.... The fundamental right of consensus is for all people to be able to express themselves in their own words and of their own will." The desired result is that groups can decide on courses of action without anyone committing the injustice of telling another person what to do. "Coercion and trade-offs are replaced with creative alternatives, and compromise with synthesis."

Now, on one hand, the lack of leaders for this group serves a practical purpose: shielding people from prosecution as ringleaders of a violent conspiracy. On the other, however, "no leaders" is what the Radical Left is all about, the rejection of archy and specifically patriarchy in preference to leaderless, consensual, anarchic sorority/fraternity.

Chapter 6

Framework for Utopia: The Individualist

That all men are by nature equally free and independent, and have certain inherent rights, of which, when they enter into a state of society, they cannot by any compact deprive or divest their posterity; namely, the enjoyment of life and liberty, with the means of acquiring and possessing property, and pursuing and obtaining happiness and safety.

George Mason
Virginia Declaration of Rights, June 12, 1776

The basic independence of the individualist consists of his loyalty to his own mind; it is his perception of the facts of reality, his understanding, his judgment, that he refuses to sacrifice to the unproved assertions of others. That is the meaning of intellectual independence—and that is the essence of an individualist.

Ayn Rand
"Counterfeit Individualism"

It might surprise many to learn that many libertarians are really rather progovernment, particularly the Individualist libertarians in the upper left of our Compass. Government, after all, provides the necessary framework for the individual's pursuit of happiness. Without a governmental framework, solitary individuals wouldn't stand a chance in the dog-eat-dog world.

The word *framework* appears often in libertarian texts. Friedrich Hayek writes that a "carefully thought-out legal framework is required" for competition to work. Milton Friedman writes that government provides "the framework within which individuals are free to pursue their own objectives." David Boaz writes that "the role of government is not to impose a particular morality but to establish a framework of rules that will guarantee each individual the freedom to pursue his own good in his own way." Virginia Postrel writes that "Dynamist rules establish a framework within which people can create nested, competing frameworks of more-specific rules."[1]

The phrase "framework for utopia" comes from Harvard's Robert Nozick, author of *Anarchy, State, and Utopia*. This 1974 libertarian classic made the case for a minimal state charged solely with protecting individuals and their sovereign rights. In libertarian terms, Nozick was a *minarchist* rather than an *anarchist*. His libertarianism was less anti-state than pro-individual.

Individualism is also the basis of the libertarianism advanced by David Boaz, executive vice president of the Cato Institute, in his book *Libertarianism: A Primer*. Boaz writes:

For libertarians, the basic unit of social analysis is the individual. It's hard to imagine how it could be anything else. Individuals are, in all cases, the source and foundation of creativity, activity, and society. Only individuals can think, love, pursue projects, act. Groups don't have plans or intentions.... Most important, only individuals can take responsibility for their actions.[2]

This is what distinguishes Individualist libertarians from all others: a singular focus on the individual, to the exclusion of all groups—family, church, tribe, class, corporation, community, race, and nation. Not all libertarians share this focus. Some libertarians are much more anti-state out of concern for the threat that the state poses to such groups. Individualists, however, are often more concerned that the state protect individuals from such groups. Their ideal society is not a group bound together by mutual obligation or archical authority, but a free association of autonomous individuals protected by an accepted legal framework.

Before going further, let's establish a useful distinction between libertarianism and individualism.

Libertarianism is a rationale for limited government based on the concept of self-ownership. The rationale assumes that every person owns his or her self, and nobody owns anybody else. Self-ownership is absolute and without political obligation (as opposed to moral or social obligation). In other words, no force may be used against a person as long as that person respects the ownership rights of others. Governments exist solely to protect said ownership rights. They may use force retributively only, to punish people for violating the ownership rights of others. Individuals also may use force, but only in self-defense. The first use of force by individuals or governments is forbidden. Libertarians of all kinds use this rationale to define strict limits on government.

Individualism, on the other hand, is a moral philosophy exalting the freedom and happiness of the individual above all else. Individualism is based on the belief that the individual alone is competent to judge what is best for him. This was the belief of many early Reformers and Levellers, who claimed for themselves the right to decide matters of faith and morals, independent of all priests and princes. It is also the belief of modern Individualists like Boaz and Hayek, who claim, as Hayek does in *The Road to Serfdom*, that "scales of value can exist only in individual minds" and therefore no scale of value can apply to all. "This is the fundamental fact on which the whole philosophy of individualism is based," Hayek writes. "It is the recognition of the individual as the ultimate judge of his ends, the belief that as far as possible his own views ought to govern his actions, that forms the essence of the individualist position."[3]

Many Individualists advocate libertarianism because it helps them justify a political regime allowing maximum personal liberty. But not all Individualists are libertarians, and not all libertarians are Individualists. Whereas libertarians are defined by their rationale for limiting the use of *kratos*, Individualists are defined by their desire to both limit *kratos* and deny *archê*. They can tolerate a particular archy when it is freely chosen and to their liking, but they resist belief in "scales of value" not of their own design.

In general, Individualists would use government to protect individuals from other individuals, but not to protect individuals from themselves or to force individuals to help others. This provides a more affirmative role for government than many people realize. The government's job is still to defend the country, catch and punish criminals, settle civil disputes, and compel parties to fulfill contracts. At a minimum, this means not only a military and a police force, but also a robust legal system to handle civil and criminal cases. For a modern capitalist economy, the legal system needs quite an elaborate body of property law setting forth clear property rights, so that assets can be used as capital. Such a system would inevitably involve government in a range of issues, from protecting the environment from pollution to protecting consumers and shareholders from negligence and fraud.

But many moderate Individualists would go much further and use force to protect individuals from discrimination on the basis of race, color, creed, sex, sexual preference, etc. Strictly speaking, such a use of force violates the libertarian principle of self-ownership by initiating force against people to make them ignore a protected condition. This deprives property owners of the free use of their property, but it also deprives individuals of their freedom of association, which compromises both their freedom of speech (by forcing people into mixed company where they must watch what they say) and their freedom of conscience (by putting the force of law behind prescribed moral choices). Even so, many Individualists back such a use of force as a desirable addition to the legal framework, on the grounds that it expands freedom and opportunity for some individuals.

Cathy Young, a contributing editor of *Reason* magazine, makes the popular distinction between equal opportunity and equal outcomes, reasoning that force is justified to provide equal opportunity but not equal outcomes. But without equal outcomes we can't really have equal opportunity, and the reason we pass laws guaranteeing equal opportunity is that we are not satisfied with the present outcomes. When asked at the Cato Institute in 2001 how laws guaranteeing equal opportunity could be justified if equal outcomes were not an appropriate goal of public policy, Young admitted in public that on this issue she is "not that libertarian."[4]

Young is not alone among moderate Individualists in being not that libertarian. When in 1996 the United States Supreme Court struck down an amendment to the Colorado state constitution prohibiting local jurisdictions from banning discrimination on the basis of homosexuality, Clint Bolick of the Institute for Justice hailed the decision as "very important in restricting all kinds of government actions. This is not about gay rights, it's about individual rights." Bolick rejoiced that the Court may have recognized "significant new restraints on majoritarian tyranny." He even praised Justice Anthony Kennedy, the author of the decision, for "quietly constructing a libertarian jurisprudence on the Court."[5]

Bolick's reaction reveals two more controversial aspects of Individualist libertarianism: its hostility to popular rule and its enthusiasm for central power. Bolick is the author of *Grassroots Tyranny*, published by the Cato Institute in 1993. The Institute for Justice is the Individualist equivalent of the American Civil Liberties Union—a public-interest law firm dedicated to defending individuals from the grassroots tyranny of state and local government. The Institute has used the courts to attack a wide range of state and local laws, from the District of Columbia's ban on street-corner shoeshine stands to the State of Texas's ban on sodomy. Often such laws are simple acts of a community's democratic will. The Colorado amendment was passed by statewide referendum and so could not have been more democratic. It was struck down by the United States Supreme Court, arguably the least democratic power in the land. But what mattered most to Bolick was that the Colorado amendment "singled out gays for hostile treatment."[6]

Neither Individualism nor libertarianism is much concerned with how political decisions are made, only with whether decisions respect individual rights. Boaz writes that the basic political issue is the relationship of the individual to the state and the most important political value is liberty, not democracy.[7] He considers democratic participation in government a "valuable safeguard for individual rights," but no guarantee that individual rights will be respected. Hayek was of the same mind:

Democracy is essentially a means, a utilitarian device for safeguarding internal peace and individual freedoms. As such it is by no means infallible or certain. Nor must we forget that there has often been much more cultural and spiritual freedom under an autocratic rule than under some democracies—and it is at least conceivable that under the government of a very homogeneous and doctrinaire majority democratic government might be as oppressive as the worst dictatorship.[8]

To the more anti-state Paleolibertarians, moderate Individualists are often no more libertarian than many Paleoconservatives. Both Indies and Paleocons believe in minimal government, but both would use that minimal government to serve their preferred freedoms. Where a Paleoconservative would allow local communities to ban sodomy, an Individualist would use the Federal Government to stop local communities from doing so.

Such enthusiasm for Big Government in the service of anti-traditional Individualism alarms Paleolibs, who see "libertarian centralism" as a threat to liberty. But there is little in Individualism against centralization, as long as the central power is dedicated to the right purposes. Ideally, Individualists would have their preferred framework cover the whole world, to give themselves all possible choice and freedom. Hayek himself wrote of the need for a worldwide federation to eliminate the pointless striving of rival nations. This, he wrote, was the hope of all right-thinking nineteenth-century liberals. "[They] may not have been fully aware *how* essential a complement of their principles a federal organization of the different states formed; but there were few among them who did not express their belief in it as an ultimate goal."[9]

In contrast to Paleolibs, who typically view all international organizations with intense suspicion, Individualists are predisposed in favor of globalization and often rather blasé about the pitfalls of international arrangements like the North American Free Trade Agreement, the World Trade Organization, and the European Union. The key is whether such arrangements provide benefits to individuals; their impact on nation-states and local cultures is not a concern.

The further we move from the center of the Compass, the more akratic Individualists become, and the more they sympathize with the extreme laissez-faire of the Libertarian Party. The self-styled "Party of Principle" does not shy away from the logical extremes of its principles. It opposes all penalties for so-called victimless crimes and would repeal all restrictions on alcohol, tobacco, firearms, explosives, drugs, gambling, prostitution, sodomy, pornography, obscenity, and suicide. It supports the separation of church and state, school and state, business and state, and bank and state. It would radically downsize government by abolishing dozens of federal agencies. It also supports "the eventual repeal of all taxation." After all, taxation requires a first use of force, which is not allowed to anyone. All public funding must therefore come from voluntary charges like user fees and court costs. Everything else is robbery.

Much of the Libertarian Party's platform reflects the influence of extreme Paleolibertarians like the late Murray Rothbard. Before he broke with the party in 1990, Rothbard was a party stalwart. He was very involved in drafting the platform, which still reads much as it did in Rothbard's day. Paleolib thinking was also represented in person by two-time Libertarian Party presidential candidate Harry Browne, author of *How I Found Freedom in an Unfree World* and *Why Government Doesn't Work*. (More on Browne in the next chapter.)

But some parts of the platform evince a more Individualist orientation. The preamble of the Libertarian Party's 2000 platform begins:

As Libertarians, we seek a world of liberty; a world in which all individuals are sovereign over their own lives, and no one is forced to sacrifice his or her values for the benefit of others.

We believe that respect for individual rights is the essential precondition for a free and prosperous world, force and fraud must be banished from human relationships, and that only through freedom can peace and prosperity be realized.

Consequently, we defend each person's right to engage in any activity that is peaceful and honest, and welcome the diversity that freedom brings. The world we seek to build is one where individuals are free to follow their own dreams in their own ways, without interference from government or any authoritarian power.[10]

Note the distinction in the last line between government and "any authoritarian power." The platform does not explain what it means by "authoritarian power," but its use of the term is a clear indication that government isn't the party's only concern. Other parts of the platform indicate that these libertarians don't much like restraint of any kind.

For example, the platform is quite critical of the military. It calls for ending the ban on homosexuals in the military, abolishing the Uniform Code of Military Justice (UCMJ), and granting military members "the same right to quit their jobs as other persons."[11] Now it could be argued upon libertarian principles that everyone in today's military is a volunteer who has signed a legal contract to obey orders and abide by the UCMJ for a limited term of service. Nevertheless, the Libertarian Party thinks the military is still too traditional and authoritarian.

The party also opposes government involvement in family life, but does not always respect parental rights. Besides conceding that child abuse sometimes warrants state intervention, the platform says that "children always have the right to establish their maturity by assuming administration and protection of their own rights, ending dependency upon their parents or other guardians, and assuming all responsibilities of adulthood."[12] Apparently, parents would have no right to stop their sons or daughters of any age from running away to live on the streets or with someone else.

The platform furthermore supports "repeal of all laws regarding consensual sexual relations, including prostitution and solicitation," without making any exception for minors or for sexual relations between family members. The crimes of statutory rape and incest would no longer exist. Neither would adultery or polygamy. Marriage itself would receive no legal sanction, since every marriage is in essence a "consensual sexual relation." Even more, the platform would bar the government from restricting private adoption services, which would effectively legalize the buying and selling of children for sexual service.[13] Whether Libertarians know it or not, their 2000 platform is a pedophile's dream.

Not all Individualists are that laissez faire in their thinking. Hayek himself wrote, "Probably nothing has done so much harm to the liberal cause as the wooden insistence of some liberals on certain rough rules of thumb, above all the principle of laissez faire."[14]

But with Rousseau, Individualists believe that man is basically good—good enough to be trusted with great freedom, which they believe will result in Nozick's libertarian Utopia. Boaz writes, "We need a limited government to usher in an unlimited future." The catch is that Utopia isn't Paradise. Boaz again:

No, a libertarian world won't be a perfect one. There will still be inequality, poverty, crime, corruption, man's inhumanity to man. But unlike the theocratic visionaries, the pie-in-the-sky socialist utopians, or the starry-eyed Mr. Fixits of the New Deal and the Great Society, libertarians don't promise you a rose garden. . . . Libertarianism holds out the goal not of a perfect society but of a freer one. It promises a world in which more of the decisions will be made in the right way by the right person: you. The result will be not an end to crime and poverty and inequality but less—often much less—of those things most of the time.[15]

Actually, some starry-eyed, visionary, utopian, libertarian Individualists do promise at least a virtual rose garden, filled with unending progress, plenty, and adventure. "We live in an enchanted world, a world suffused with intelligence, a world of our making. In such plentitude, too, lies an adventurous future," writes Virginia Postrel, ex-editor-in-chief of *Reason* magazine, in her book *The Future and Its Enemies: The Growing Conflict Over Creativity, Enterprise, and Progress.*[16]

Postrel sees the world divided into two warring camps: *dynamists* who welcome change and *stasists* who hate it. Stasists are further divided into *reactionaries* who want to lock in the past and *technocrats* who want to lock in the future. But these are all just new names for old actors: dynamists are libertarians, reactionaries are conservatives, and technocrats are liberals. Postrel is merely accentuating the positive of her own position, founded upon the progressive power of libertarian Individualism. Instead of running down government, she is playing up the individual's heroic potential. All the usual themes are there: liberty, equality, diversity, and the future:

There is in fact no single future: "the" future encompasses the many microfutures of individuals and their associations. . . . How we feel about the evolving future tells us who we are as individuals and as a civilization: Do we search for *stasis*—a regulated, engineered world? Or do we embrace *dynamism*—a world of constant creation, discovery, and competition? Do we value stability and control, or evolution and learning?[17]

There aren't many rules in the dynamist world. The few that Postrel outlines are, in so many words, the standard libertarian guarantees of life, liberty, property, expression, and protection within a legal framework to settle disputes and enforce contracts. These rules serve an "open society" and an "open-ended future." They "let people forge new bonds, invent new institutions, and find better ways of doing things." They "allow us to create the bonds of life—to turn the atoms of our individual selves, our ideas, and the stuff of our material world into the complex social, intellectual, and technological molecules that make up our civilization."[18]

Postrel talks a lot about individuals and civilization but says nearly nothing of families, churches, corporations, communities, races, or nations. When she does talk of groups, she favors groups without leaders, namely flocks of birds, ant colonies, and the Internet. Others have talked of bees (Bernard Mandeville) and an invisible hand (Adam Smith). Postrel doesn't mention these, but her point is the same: free individuals create their own order as they pursue their own interests. Postrel does mention Hayek many times and uses his words to describe her dynamists as "the party of life, the party that favors free growth and spontaneous evolution."[19]

Postrel tells us, "The dynamist moral vision, then, emphasizes individual flourishing and individual responsibility. It sees human nature fulfilled in learning, creating, and adapting to the world." The result is a glorious diversity of endeavors:

A dynamist world has room for a wide range of enterprises: for both Promise Keepers and *Ms.*, for the macho culture of Intel and the zaniness of Southwest Airlines, for Web sites devoted to biblical exegesis and Web sites devoted to pornography, for punks and debutantes, Mozart and Madonna, *The Little Mermaid* and *Pulp Fiction.*[20]

This is all well and good with dynamists, who are always learning but never coming to a knowledge of unchanging truth. Individualists often stop short of such claims. They are not quite relativists, for they reserve for themselves the right to reject what they don't like. But most often they talk only of what should be allowed under an ideal legal framework. "Rights theory can't tell us what moral obligations we ought to feel toward family members," Boaz admits. "Libertarianism is a political philosophy, not a complete moral code. It prescribes certain minimal rules for living together in a peaceful, productive society—property, contract, and freedom—and leaves further moral teaching to civil society."[21]

For their part, Individualists don't have much good to say about moral teaching. Hayek condemns at length "collectivist ethics" that impose a "complete ethical code." "No such complete ethical code exists," he insists. Boaz dodges the question of whether unborn babies have a "right to life." "Obviously, that is not the sense in which Jefferson used the term," he writes. "We might do better to stick to 'right to self-ownership.'" On the same issue, the Party of Principle turns uncharacteristically pragmatic. It opposes funding for abortion on the grounds that some people believe abortion to be murder, but also opposes government doing anything about such alleged murders. It seems that one's rights as an individual depend on someone else's labor. Call it the Labor Theory of Human Value.[22]

This reluctance to make moral judgments is why everyone else around the Compass suspects that these libertarians are just libertines who don't believe in right or wrong but push libertarianism because it would let them to do as they please. Few Individualists believe in God. One poll of Libertarian Party supporters found that only 27 percent believe in God, though 97 percent of Americans did. The poll's authors noted that "many libertarians are not only areligious, but militantly antireligious, as indicated by extensive write-in comments." Libertarian causes often include among their supporters people like John Stagliano, maker of hardcore skin flicks, reader of *Reason* magazine, and contributor to the Cato Institute, the Libertarian Party, and the Drug Policy Foundation.[23]

Even some Individualists judge such libertarians harshly. The atheistic followers of Ayn Rand have been especially critical of them. To Randians, libertarianism is not a philosophy because it claims no single basis in truth. It is instead a bare-bones political program, justified in different ways by different people. Many libertarians go no further philosophically than the assertion of individual rights. Some ground their rights in religion, but many others are philosophic skeptics, moral subjectivists, and social anarchists. Randians consider all of these positions inconsistent with reason, order, and freedom. One has written of libertarianism's "perversion of liberty." Rand herself refused the libertarian label and instead called herself a "radical for capitalism."

What libertarianism lacks, Rand tried to provide with her own philosophy of objectivism. Objectivism, quite literally, makes selfishness a virtue, defining selfishness as the rational pursuit of one's own well-being. This is not a license to do as you please, however, for Rand considered many things such as homosexuality and feminism to be irrational. Reason, she believed, saves selfishness from subjectivism. Rand despised Christianity as an irrational and thus immoral superstition. Objectivism was her antidote to the immorality of Christian humility and self-sacrifice. "My philosophy, in essence, is the concept of man as a heroic being, with his own happiness as the moral purpose of his life, with productive achievement as his noblest activity, and reason as his only absolute."[24]

Whether Rand's objectivism succeeds in avoiding subjectivism is an open question. Her "only absolute" has led many of her followers to reject her judgments on homosexuality and feminism on the grounds that Rand didn't have all the facts. Randians have reasoned differently also in the struggle against Islamic fundamentalism. Some have opposed the war in Iraq, citing Rand's own opposition to Korea, Vietnam, and World Wars I and II. Others—including her disciples at the Ayn Rand Institute, the Objectivist Center, and *Reason* magazine—have welcomed the Iraq War and the broader War on Terror as rational responses to the threat of irrational and anti-liberal Islam. One side cites Rand's warnings about the "New Fascism" she believed was responsible for fomenting war abroad; the other side, recalling Rand's endorsement of "national self-interest" and her condemnation of Palestinian terrorists as "savages," has laid aside complaints about the state's part in stirring Islamic extremism and rationalized a new colonialism to spread the gospel of rational self-interest to the Middle East and Eastern Europe.[25]

It is not clear which side Rand herself would have taken, but since 9-11 the weight of objectivist and Individualist opinion has been for war. Most leading Individualists have either kept quiet like David Boaz or signed on in support like Virginia Postrel. At the Cato Institute, aggressive globalists Tom Palmer and Brink Lindsey are in, and anti-interventionists Ivan Eland and Charles Peña are out. Eland is now at the libertarian Independent Institute; Peña is a fellow of the Coalition for a Realistic Foreign Policy (CRFP). Cato helped to found the CRFP, but from the start the coalition was compromised by a general reluctance to implicate Israel and by the sympathy of many coalition members for the Bush administration's stated goal of "global democratic revolution." They disagree with Bush on the matter of means but not of ends.

Among the handful of idealistic Individualists holding fast to the upper left's akratic creed, perhaps the best known and most colorful is Justin Raimondo, the taboo-busting editorial director of Antiwar.com. Raimondo started out like many Individualists as a fan of Ayn Rand. As a teen, he imitated Rand by changing his first name from Dennis to Justin, a supremely Individualist act. (Rand's birth name was Alissa Rosenbaum.) After a brief involvement with Young Americans for Freedom, Raimondo joined the Libertarian Party, co-founding a "Radical Caucus" that allied him with party main-brain Murray Rothbard. Dissatified with the party's direction and fortunes, Raimondo defected to the Reagan GOP in 1983, founding the Libertarian Republican Organizing Committee to try to bring other libertarians with him. Dissatisfied again with the post-Reagan GOP, Raimondo joined Rothbard in the John Randolph Club, which cheered on Pat Buchanan's 1992 Republican revolt against President George H.W. Bush. Raimondo backed Buchanan again in 1996 and 2000, then Ralph Nader in 2004. He ran for Congress as a Republican in 1996 against Democrat Nancy Pelosi, but won only 13 percent of the vote.

Raimondo's stock and store is hyper-Menckenian mockery of his pro-war opponents—neoconservatives first of all, followed by libertarian globalists, Zionist Christians, and establishment liberals. His columns are peppered with derisive epithets like "chickenhawk" and "laptop bombardier" and liberally laced with links to supporting material. He has written damningly of the "Objectivist death cult" and daringly of "Likudniks" in America and Israel, whom he blames for 9-11 and its aftermath. Such criticism has naturally earned him the accusation of antisemitism, another Menckenian trait, but one which Raimondo denies, insisting that his complaint is against Israeli and American imperialists, not against Jews or Israelis per se. Raimondo's longtime friend and dot-com collaborator Eric Garris is himself Jewish, and their Web site features a regular column by Israeli libertarian Ran HaCohen. In fact, Raimondo was anti-state and anti-war long before Israel entered the picture. He founded Antiwar.com in 1995 to oppose American military intervention in Bosnia, and he achieved national notoriety during the Kosovo war. Before 9-11, Raimondo was just as likely to be accused of anti-Islamism as antisemitism for often reminding his Web site readers of the militant Islam of the NATO's Bosnian and Albanian partners.

Raimondo's anti-war monomania makes his personal perspective difficult to identify based solely on his published works. His organizational attachments are to the Right. He is a contributing editor of *The American Conservative* and a former adjunct scholar at the Ludwig von Mises Institute. Antiwar.com is a project of the Center for Libertarian Studies, which also funds the plainly Paleolibertarian sister-site LewRockwell.com. But the openly gay Raimondo has been far more open than most Paleolibertarians to bridging the Left/Right divide by embracing Radical leftists like Alexander Cockburn, once a regular Antiwar.com columnist, and Gore Vidal, of whom Raimondo has many times expressed admiration.

To be sure, Vidal, of late, has written enough against the "warfare state" to almost qualify as at least an honorary Paleolibertarian. Reviewing Vidal's *Inventing a Nation* for *The American Conservative*, Raimondo identifies Vidal's perspective as that of the "proto-libertarian" George Mason, the anti-Federalist author of the Bill of Rights.[26] In his own words, Vidal laments "the collapse of the idea of the citizen as someone autonomous whose private life is not subject to orders from above." He warns that "our garrison state is now turning inward to create a police state." He recommends "moving boldly forward into the past," where he finds the example of Henry Clay, whom he lauds as an "America Firster."[27]

But a longing for the past is also characteristic of many Radicals. Vidal is easier to classify as a nostalgic Radical than the libertarian patriot Raimondo imagines, but he does often give evidence of Individualist inclinations. "Temperamentally, I am suspicious of belonging to anything," Vidal wrote many years ago. "I have always been a conservative cross borne sadly by liberal friends. I began life as an absolute monarchist, on condition of course that I be that monarch."[28]

Only in the upper left do we find a great divide between moderates and extremists. In every other corner the two are much more sympathetic, but among Individualists the philosophical focus on self-interest subjects the psyche to severe tension between concern for personal welfare and commitment to Individualist principle. What, after all, is a rational Individualist to do when the crowd about him is shouting *Sieg heil*? The guiding light of self-interest gives him little reason to stand on principle in the face of persecution. More often it compromises his commitment to ideals and inclines him toward self-serving pragmatism. In bad times, he may find it in his interest to rebel against oppressive others, but in good times, all too often, a vortex of self-interest pulls him down and right, where money and power are most often found. Extreme Individualists like Raimondo are far enough out to escape the pull; moderate Individualists like Postrel and Palmer and Lindsey are not.

Chapter 7

Breaking the Clock: The Paleolibertarian

The few haughty Families, think They *must govern. The Body of the People tamely consent & submit to be their Slaves. This unravels the Mystery of Millions being enslaved by the few!*

Samuel Adams
Letter to Richard Henry Lee, 1787

There is an alternative to the Politically Correct Left and the Militarized Right: . . . there is freedom itself, the genuine article, and a tradition of thought in defense of freedom unmatched by any other in its rigor and dedication.

Llewellyn H. Rockwell Jr.
"Speak the Truth," 2001

By the end of the eighties, Lew Rockwell had had enough. He had never been much a part of the Libertarian Party (LP) until Congressman Ron Paul of Texas decided to run for president as a Libertarian in 1988. Rockwell had worked for Paul on Capitol Hill and rallied behind him to help secure his nomination. Friends of Rockwell, close ideological allies like Murray Rothbard, had been active in the LP for years, but even the Paul campaign could not bring Rockwell into the fold for good. In the January 1990 issue of *Liberty* magazine, Rockwell let everyone know why.

Libertarianism, Rockwell wrote, needed to be "deloused." The LP had "smeared the most glorious political idea in human history with libertine muck." It had equated freedom from State oppression with freedom from bourgeois morality, cultural norms, and Christian religion. It had avoided issues of great importance to average Americans like civil rights, crime, and environmentalism. It had joined the Left in trashing the values that most Americans held dear:

When the LP nominates a prostitute for lieutenant governor of California and she becomes a much-admired LP celebrity, how can regular Americans help but think that libertarianism is hostile to social norms, or that legalization of such acts as prostitution means moral approval? There could be no more political suicidal or morally fallacious connection, but the LP has forged it.[1]

Rockwell rejected the notion that libertarianism was strictly a political doctrine with nothing to say about morality and culture. No political philosophy exists in a "cultural vacuum," he wrote. "The family, the free market, the dignity of the individual, private property rights, the very concept of freedom—all are products of our religious culture. . . . Christianity gave birth to individualism by stressing the significance of the single soul. . . . Christianity made possible the development of capital." Yet the LP's culture was "anti-religious, modernist, morally relativist, and egalitarian." This anti-religious tone has "helped keep libertarianism such a small movement."

It was time, Rockwell declared, to "discard the defective cultural framework of libertarianism" and offer the American people a respectable alternative. Not a new alternative, he wrote, but an old one, harking back to its roots among pre-war, pre-Rand proto-libertarians such as H. L. Mencken and Albert Jay Nock: "I call my suggested replacement, with its ethically-based cultural principles, 'paleolibertarianism': the old libertarianism."

Paleolibertarianism combined conservative social values with the laissez-faire economics of the so-called Austrian School. Individualists also look to the Austrian School for their economics, but whereas the Indies' favorite Austrian is the moderate Friedrich Hayek (1899–1992), the Paleolibs' favorite is the more extreme Ludwig von Mises (1881–1973). Rockwell is founder and president of the Ludwig von Mises Institute; Murray Rothbard, until his death in 1995, was Mises's leading champion.

Some leading libertarians opposed Rockwell's founding of the Ludwig von Mises Institute in 1982 on the grounds that Mises and Rothbard were too radical. Charles Koch of Koch Industries had thrown his wealth behind the Cato Institute in Washington, D.C., with the aim of working libertarian ideas into the political mainstream. That meant concentrating on economics and avoiding explosive social issues like civil rights, which conservative libertarians like Rockwell were not content to do. As they saw it, mainstream libertarians were too pleased with the general drift of

American politics and culture, which was freeing up sexual behavior but taking away age-old freedoms to speak and act on differences of race, religion, and gender.

To be sure, Mises himself was no conservative. His theory was entirely materialistic and individualistic. But the leftward drift of American politics and culture gave cultural conservatives more cause to be anti-state than progressive libertarians. At the same time, conservative complaints gave Misesian individualists even more to lay against the State. The result was a convergence of Left and Right anti-statists in the Paleolibertarian position. This convergence was incarnate in the persons of Murray Rothbard and Lew Rockwell.

Murray Rothbard's father was an independent-minded Jewish immigrant whose faith in American freedom resisted the family's Communist sympathies. In his younger days, Rothbard was briefly a disciple of Ayn Rand, but he married a Christian woman and later broke with Rand over Rand's failed attempts to convert his wife to atheism. His real roots were in the Old Right of the 1930s, as represented by H. L. Mencken, Albert Jay Nock, Rose Wilder Lane, Isabel Patterson, Frank Chodorov, and Garet Garrett. Further back, he looked to American anarchists like Lysander Spooner and Benjamin Tucker and progressive individualists like Herbert Spencer, Henry David Thoreau, Frederic Bastiat, Thomas Jefferson, Thomas Paine, and John Locke. An agnostic, Rothbard nevertheless believed strongly in natural rights. He was against both the New Deal and the Cold War and blamed "hysterical anticommunism" for compromising the Old Right's libertarian principles. Over the years, he assumed an increasingly favorable view of Christianity, even writing that "everything good in Western civilization, from individual liberty to the arts, is due to Christianity." He was never comfortable with the word *conservative* but did often describe himself as "right-wing radical."

Lew Rockwell's father was also of the Old Right—a Republican supporter of Ohio Senator Robert A. Taft. Like many on the Old Right, Rockwell was against the Vietnam War. He was a "reluctant Goldwaterite" in 1964 and worked briefly for Eugene McCarthy in 1968. Though a generation younger than Rothbard, Rockwell's list of influences is much the same: Mencken, Nock, Lane, Chodorov, Garrett, and John T. Flynn. His economic thinking began with Henry Hazlitt and continued with the Austrian School, eventually making him, in his own words, a "thoroughgoing Misesian."[2] But unlike Rothbard, whose organizational ties were to the left, among libertarians, Rockwell kept company with conservatives. He worked as a book editor for Neil McCaffrey, a Roman Catholic traditionalist who was the founder of Arlington House publishing company and the Conservative

Book Club. Rockwell started Hillsdale College's publishing house and its quarterly newsletter *Imprimis*. He later went to work for Ron Paul, during Paul's first tour in Congress as a Republican.

Rockwell's broadside against the libertarian movement forced a realignment. Rothbard broke with the Libertarian Party and later resigned as a senior editor of *Liberty* magazine. Together they sought out an alliance with the Paleoconservatives of the anti-government Right. In 1990, the Paleolibs at the Ludwig von Mises Institute and the Center for Libertarian Studies joined the Paleocons of the Rockford Institute to form the John Randolph Club, named after the early American Virginia aristocrat who was equally anti-federal and anti-egalitarian. The new club's motto, adopted at Rockwell's suggestion, was Randolph's declaration "I love liberty; I hate equality."

The John Randolph Club got off to a rousing start, boosted by Patrick Buchanan's 1992 rebellion against President George Bush. At a club dinner that year, outside Washington, D.C., Rothbard attacked William F. Buckley Jr. for purging the conservative movement of its radical elements, both libertarian and traditionalist. Against the "cultural Marxists" who argue that we can't turn back the clock, Rothbard declared his intention not to turn it back, but to break it:

With the inspiration of the death of the Soviet Union before us, we now know that it can be done. We shall break the clock of social democracy. We shall break the clock of the Great Society. We shall break the clock of the welfare state. We shall break the clock of the New Deal. We shall break the clock of Woodrow Wilson's New Freedom and perpetual war. We shall repeal the twentieth century.[3]

But the Paleo alliance peaked early, not long thereafter. The Paleolibs were increasingly dismayed by Buchanan's economic populism, and the Paleocons never lost their suspicion of Misesian materialism. Rothbard's death in 1995 deprived the alliance of its dominant personality, without which it fell apart. In the end, the alliance proved even less successful than the "fusionism" of the 1960s, which led to the founding of the Philadelphia Society as a bridge between anti-socialist libertarians like Milton Friedman and anti-communist conservatives like Buckley.

Today Rockwell's Paleolibertarianism is still the intellectual lodestar for the anti-statists at the top of our Compass, but we'll use the term a bit more broadly, applying it to the range of anti-government sentiment stretching due north of dead center. After all, long before anyone ever heard of the Austrian School, there was the Federal Government, stealing power from the states, extending and strengthening its reach across the mountains and the plains, and drawing more and more of life into its New Deal net. All along there was resistance to it among the hardy souls who got along well enough without Uncle Sam and mightily resented his unsought "help."

Such a soul was Rose Wilder Lane (1886–1968), journalist, novelist, and polemicist for freedom. Lane was the daughter of Laura Ingalls Wilder, author of the "Little House" series of children's books, which inspired the television series "Little House on the Prairie." Lane had grown up in that little house and remembered it fondly. Though the struggle to survive on the prairie ruined her father's health, the spirit of self-reliance was bred into her. Her belief in frontier individualism and the evils of government grew stronger with the years. In 1938, she described her personal evolution with these words:

Politically, I cast my first vote—on a sample ballot—for [Grover] Cleveland, at the age of three. I was an ardent if uncomprehending Populist; I saw America ruined forever when the soulless corporations in 1896 defeated [William Jennings] Bryan and Free Silver. I was a Christian Socialist with [Eugene] Debs, and distributed untold numbers of the Appeal to Reason. From 1914 to 1920—when I first went to Europe—I was a pacifist; innocently, if criminally, I thought war stupid, cruel, wasteful and unnecessary. I voted for [Woodrow] Wilson because he kept us out of it.

In 1917 I became a convinced, though not practicing communist. In Russia, for some reason, I wasn't and I said so, but my understanding of [Bolshevism] made everything pleasant when the Cheka arrested me a few times.

I am now a fundamentalist American; give me time and I will tell you why individualism, laissez faire and the slightly restrained anarchy of capitalism offer the best opportunities for the development of the human spirit. Also I will tell you why the relative freedom of human spirit is better—and more productive, even in material ways—than the communist, Fascist, or any other rigidity organized for material ends.[4]

Lane begins life as a progressive populist striving against the "soulless corporations" of the Republican establishment. But when the Left triumphs to become the new establishment—in Russia under the Bolsheviks and in the United States under Franklin Roosevelt—Lane's thinking takes a libertarian turn. In the last paragraph, she sounds many themes common to Indies and Paleolibs, but it's the government that she's against, not the social groups so necessary to survival on the frontier. She shares Ayn Rand's faith in radical capitalism, but not Rand's rationalism, materialism, or Christophobia. Her individualism is neither progressive nor misanthropic. It does not resist identification with the past or with all groups. Lane traveled widely through Europe and the Middle East, and lived for a while in San

Francisco and New York, but when success brought her the wherewithal to live wherever she wanted, she made her home on a farm in the Missouri Ozarks. Try imagining Ayn Rand in the Ozarks.

In some ways, the difference between Indies and Paleolibs is a difference between city libertarians and country libertarians. City libs are proudly progressive and anti-traditional. They look down on the old ways still kept in the country and enjoy the city's material abundance, diverse social mix, moral latitude, and protective legal system. In contrast, country libs prefer small towns, family ties, and accustomed ways, with a neighborly allowance for the eccentricities that grow up naturally among free and self-reliant folk, absent interference from far-off officials. Instead of expanding the legal framework to higher levels, they would rather keep government small and local, so that it won't get out of hand.

A deep distrust of big government lies in the heart of all Paleolibs. They are localists and decentralists by nature, more anti-state than pro-individual. Whereas Indies often look to the State to protect the individual, Paleolibs would rather that society were governed entirely by the akratic social order than by the coercive political order. They are therefore much more bothered than Individualists by anti-discrimination laws, which are destructive of natural, akratic social archies. Hans-Hermann Hoppe, editor of the *Journal of Libertarian Studies* and a student of Murray Rothbard, writes:

Forced integration is a means of breaking up all intermediate social institutions and hierarchies (in between the state and the individual) such as family, clan, tribe, community, and church and their internal layers and ranks of authority. In so doing the individual is isolated (atomized) and its power of resistance vis-a-vis the state weakened.[5]

This anti-government sentiment appears in populist form in the mind-your-own-business attitude of many Western Republicans. "Never believe it when someone says, 'I'm from the government and I'm here to help,'" says former House Majority Leader Dick Armey of Texas. "Free people do not give up their freedom easily, and governments know that. That's why governments have become so skillful in using pretensions of altruism when they try to take a measure of our freedom away from us."[6]

No one used such words to greater effect than Ronald Reagan, who declared in his first inaugural address that "government is not the solution to our problem; government is the problem." Reagan was raised in the Midwest and strongly identified with the frontier spirit of the Old West. Three times he ran for president against the East Coast business establishment of the Republican Party, which backed Richard Nixon in 1968, Gerald Ford in 1976, and George Bush in 1980. A part of the Reagan spirit survives today in the Republican Party's "leave-us-alone coalition" of libertarians, social conservatives, and free-marketeers, all of which want government to get out of their lives.

The trick is translating the general anti-government animus into a coherent political philosophy. That's where the coalition often breaks down. For Paleolibs, the answer is conservative libertarianism, aptly outlined by Rockwell in his 1990 manifesto. Rockwell listed ten articles of faith embraced by virtually all Paleolibs, with more or less ardor. In Rockwell's words, Paleolibs see—

1. The leviathan State as the institutional source of evil throughout history.
2. The unhampered free market as a moral and practical imperative.
3. Private property as an economic and moral necessity for a free society.
4. The garrison State as a preeminent threat to liberty and social well-being.
5. The welfare State as organized theft that victimizes producers and eventually even its "clients."
6. Civil liberties based on property rights as essential to a just society.
7. The egalitarian ethic as morally reprehensible and destructive of private property and social authority.
8. Social authority—as embodied in the family, church, community, and other intermediating institutions—as helping protect the individual from the State and necessary for a free and virtuous society.
9. Western culture as eminently worthy of preservation and defense.
10. Objective standards of morality, especially as found in the Judeo-Christian tradition, as essential to the free and civilized social order.[7]

Rockwell writes, "The libertarian must agree with the first six points, but most activists [being Individualists] will be outraged by the last four. Yet there is nothing unlibertarian in them." All libertarians accept the basic libertarian program of private property and individual rights, and so there is considerable crossover among Indies and Paleolibs supporting the same organizations and writing for the same magazines. They differ greatly, however, on the larger issues of community, culture, ethics, and religion, and this is apparent in their preferred themes.

Open any issue of *Reason* magazine and you will find more than a few very un-Paleo ads and articles: Nick Gillespie defending medical marijuana, Jacob Sullum giving a thumbs-down to controls on Internet porn, Ronald Bailey taking pokes at Neoconservatives for encouraging doubts about evolution, Charles Paul Freund writing "In Praise of Vulgarity: How Commercial Culture Liberates Islam—and the West," or an advocate of "unschooling" decrying the blackboard tyranny of organized education: "People learn passivity [in the classroom]. People are controlled and become accustomed to control. So it constricts people into not thinking for themselves, not making choices for themselves, and not imagining very large possibilities for themselves and for the world."[8]

What you won't find in *Reason* are many articles addressing some favorite Paleolib issues: Walter E. Williams defending the Southern Confederacy and the Confederate battle flag; the Reverend Robert Sirico of the Acton Institute making the Catholic case for capitalism; M. Stanton Evans praising the Christian faith of the founding fathers; Paul Craig Roberts denouncing racial quotas; or the renegade Lew Rockwell writing about anything. Among the thirty-five "Heroes of Freedom" named in *Reason*'s thirty-fifth anniversary issue, the editors included porn peddler Larry Flynt for "helping to strengthen First Amendment protections," tennis star Martina Navratilova for "smash[ing] stultifying stereotypes," and basketball bizarro Dennis Rodman for "challeng[ing] the lantern-jawed stiffness that had traditionally made sports stars such dull role models."[9] They also included Czech progressive Vaclav Havel who "pushed artistic boundaries [and] defended the right of rock stars to be filthy," thereby supposedly bringing down communism. Paleolibs would have preferred Havel's conservative libertarian rival, Vaclav Klaus, and would never have mentioned the other three except in scorn.[10]

It often happens that people within a movement agree on the desired *ends*, but not the *means* for achieving them. This is true of Paleolibs and Paleocons: They agree on the civilizational ends, but not on the libertarian means. The reverse is true of Paleolibs and Indies: They agree on the libertarian means, but not on the civilizational ends.

The importance of tradition and religion to the Paleo form of libertarianism receives a full defense from veteran conservative journalist Stan Evans in his 1994 book *The Theme Is Freedom: Religion, Politics, and the American Tradition.* Evans was a student of Mises, but a disciple of the late Frank Meyer, champion of *fusionism*, a synthesis of libertarian politics and Christian (or Judeo-Christian) tradition. In *The Theme Is Freedom*, Evans names Meyer as his nearest intellectual kin, but he rejects the fusionist label "emphatically." Meyer also disliked it. For both men, no fusion is needed:

The point is not that liberty and religious value [*sic*] can be "fused" by some ingenious method, but rather that they are a necessary unity—hemispheres that form a whole, thematically and in the development of our institutions. Western freedom is the product of our faith, and the precepts of that faith are essential to its survival.[11]

Much that Evans writes would also suit the Paleocons or Theocons. Political liberty and Christian religion are inseparable. Virtue is a must in a free society. We owe our freedoms to our Anglo-American tradition, not rational abstraction. No other tradition has placed more stress on personal liberty and limited government. Moral relativism is "the central fallacy of liberal thought." Atheism and freedom are antithetical, for, "Loss of belief goes hand in hand with loss of self-reliance, and thus the rise of statist practice." The American founders understood this and conceived the United States as a Christian nation.[12]

But, as the book's title makes plain, Evans's main theme is political freedom. The founders, he writes, were most concerned to limit government, not to overthrow all limits on personal behavior, but to minimize the evil effects of power. They believed that power corrupts and that virtue requires freedom, just as freedom requires virtue. The best course is to limit power and look to the rule of law to preserve accustomed liberties. "A regime of liberty under law, as they conceived it, could by no means guarantee morality. But it could prevent some of the grossest *im*morality—the suffering and coercion that despotism imposes on its victims."[13]

Evans welcomes the political involvement of the Religious Right, which he says is less a threat to freedom than a victim of government, on the defensive against a "secularist blitzkrieg in the schools and other public institutions."[14] He goes to great lengths to show the religious roots of the American tradition, discoursing with apparent approval on the use of religious oaths by the states. He writes that the First Amendment was a bar upon the central government, not the states, and that its anti-establishment clause does not erect a "wall of separation" between government and religion. And yet he stops short of endorsing any specific involvement of government in religion. If public schools are anti-religious, the solution is to get the government out of education.

Evans recommends a low profile for the United States in the world and a "determined rollback of federal power across the board, when and wherever this can be accomplished."[15] Admitting a risk of overstatement, he writes that "anything which can decrease the power of the federal government should be encouraged."[16] He rejects the ambitions of "Tory paternalists" who would use the state to attempt too much. That is not the American way, he writes:

... the chief political tradition of our culture *is*, above all else, a tradition of limited government, in the interest of protecting personal freedom.... The oft-stated conflict between traditional values and libertarian practice in our politics is therefore an illusion—a misreading of the record, or an artifact of special pleading. In the Anglo-American context, "big government conservatism" is the oxymoron—whatever its vogue among paternalists in Europe.[17]

He positions himself midway between "traditionalist-paternalists" like Joseph de Maistre and "classical liberals" like Herbert Spencer and John Stuart Mill: "My view, of course, is that each side of this argument had it half right: Maistre on issues of religion and tradition, Mill and Spencer on state power and personal freedom. Combine the halves and you have, essentially, Lord Acton."[18]

Further up on the K scale, the animus against government intensifies, yet still we find a conservative inclination. The late Libertarian Party presidential candidate Harry Browne begins his 1996 campaign book *Why Government Doesn't Work* with a patently conservative appeal:

Imagine living in a city where you felt safe walking home at ten in the evening—or even two in the morning.

Imagine your children going to schools that respect your values; where teachers concentrate on reading, writing, adding, subtracting, and other academic basics; where no one would dare teach your child a philosophy that's alien to you.

Imagine paying only half the taxes you're paying now. . . .

I'm not describing Utopia. Such a society wouldn't be perfect. But as recently as 1950, it was real. The crime rate was only one fifth of what it is today. Most American school children learned to read, write, and do math competently—and they left school able to make their way in the world. Government was only one fifth the size it is today.[19]

Browne is convinced that the difference between the 1950s and now is government. There was less then; there is more now. "The decline of America has been caused by politicians and reformers who believe that you aren't competent to run your own life," he writes. He is also convinced that nearly nothing government does turns out right: "To run your life for you, they have created a government that fails at everything it undertakes, but wants to undertake everything."[20]

Browne defines government as an "agency of coercion." He defines coercion as "the use of force and the threat of force to win obedience." Everything government does is backed by force, from helping flood victims to mandating family-leave policies at work. "When someone asks for a government program, he is saying in effect, 'Tell the police to use their guns to get me what I want.'" He writes:

Of course, there are other agencies of coercion—such as the Mafia. So to be more precise, government is the agency of coercion that has flags in front of its offices.

Or, to put it another way, government is society's dominant producer of coercion. The Mafia and independent bandits are merely fringe competitors—seeking to take advantage of the niches and nooks neglected by the government.[21]

Browne is all for defending the country but thinks the country would not much need defending if it were not so imperialistic. He would not have led the United States into any war since the Revolution—even World War II, which "made the world safe for Joseph Stalin." War is "just one more government program," inefficiently run like the U.S. Postal Service. Government doesn't work, even when fighting wars. "If it wins a war, it's only because it's fighting another government."[22]

Like most Paleocons and many Paleolibs, Browne actually looks rather fondly on the United States before the Civil War. Until then, the federal government had made only "brief, self-conscious excursions outside its Constitutional limits." The Civil War was the first of four fateful periods of "wholesale looting of freedom." The three other periods were the Progressive Era (1900–1918), the New Deal (1929–1945), and the Great Society (1961–1975). Together these calamities "destroyed the qualities that had made America unique" and "transformed America from a free country into a nation of obedient serfs, paper-pushers, victims, whiners, and antagonists."[23]

At some point on the K scale, Paleolibertarians do indeed become anarchists of a sort, though their preferred term is "anarcho-capitalists." *Akratic* capitalists or simply *akratists* would be more accurate. Both terms avoid confusion with the anti-archy Radicals at the left end of the A scale. Paleolibs, after all, are not so much against *archê* as *kratos*—the State's monopoly on the use of force.

Anarchic Radicals and akratic Paleolibs share many characteristics. Both are idealistic contrarians at odds with the Establishment, especially as represented by the plutocratic Neoconservatives of the lower right. Both see the "War on Terror" as a Neocon vehicle for expanding the American empire and defending Israel. Both have protested Israeli influence in U.S. policymaking and generally sympathized with the Muslim world's complaints against Israel and the United States. Most Individualists have confined their complaints to the sacrifice of civil liberties at home and warnings about the costs and risks of military intervention. Many have publicly backed the use of force abroad, with little sympathy for Muslim sensibilities.

But while the Radicals' bugbears are tradition, patriarchy, and the Corporations, the Paleolibs' are—left to right—democratic socialism and democratic capitalism. These are the two wings of what Paleolibs sometimes call the "War Party." Both are inclined toward crusading imperialism in the name of freedom and democracy. Both are viewed by akratic Paleolibs as fundamentally dishonest justifications for the tyranny of what Rothbard called "the welfare/warfare state."

Democracy itself is suspect, to say the least. "If one must have a state," writes Hans-Hermann Hoppe in his 2001 book *Democracy: The God That Failed*, "then it is economically and ethically advantageous to choose monarchy over democracy." The monarchy Hoppe has in mind is a limited monarchy based on private property, with the monarch as the major property owner. The advantage is that property owners are better stewards of their estates than temporarily elected officials, who promise more than they can deliver to get elected, without much concern for the long term. Hoppe argues that the "private ownership of the governmental apparatus of compulsion (monarchy)" is the most reliable and most natural form of government, "for who would not rather trust a specific known individual . . . than an anonymous, democratically elected person?"[24]

But Hoppe is not a monarchist. He would rather have no government, for all governments are coercive. "The power to tax . . . is ethically unacceptable," he writes. The State is a "monopolist of ultimate decisionmaking," and, as with every monopolist, its decisions are insulated from correction by the market. This "monopolist of ultimate decisionmaking equipped with the power to tax does not just produce less and lower quality justice, but he will produce more and more 'bads,' i.e., injustice and aggression."[25]

The ideal is a "social system free from monopoly and taxation." This Hoppe calls "natural order." He writes, "Other names used elsewhere or by others to refer to the same thing include 'ordered anarchy,' 'private property anarchism,' 'anarcho-capitalism,' 'autogovernment,' 'private law society,' and 'pure capitalism.'"[26] Or, we might say, *akrateia*—the utter absence of coercive force in human affairs.

Chapter 8

For the Permanent Things: The Paleoconservative

We are descended from a people whose government was founded on liberty; our glorious forefathers of Great Britain made liberty the foundation of everything. That country is become a great, mighty, and splendid nation; not because their government is strong and energetic, but, sir, because liberty is its direct end and foundation. We drew the spirit of liberty from our British ancestors; by that spirit we have triumphed over every difficulty.

Patrick Henry
Virginia Ratification Convention, 1788

This struggle to preserve the old creeds, cultures, and countries of the West is the new divide between Left and Right; this struggle will define what it means to be a conservative. This is the cause of the twenty-first century and the agenda of conservatism for the remainder of our lives.

Patrick J. Buchanan
The Death of the West, 2002

For many American conservatives, the "Reagan Revolution" in 1980 could only have been surpassed by the Second Coming of Christ. "At last, the Silent Majority had spoken! It had come to its senses and repudiated liberalism," recalls Joseph Sobran, who was then a senior editor of *National Review.* "Suddenly, the prescribed tone for conservatives was optimism; happy days were here again! The aloof pessimism of the original movement was forgotten."[1]

But for conservatives of Sobran's sentiments, the disappointments started early. They suffered a signal defeat when the new White House passed over M.E. Bradford to head the National Endowment of the Humanities. Bradford was a distinguished scholar of English literature at the University of Dallas and a respected Southern conservative, whose candidacy was backed by William F. Buckley Jr. and several Southern senators, Republican and Democrat. But Bradford had backed George Wallace in 1968 and 1972 and written damningly of Abraham Lincoln as a murderous tyrant who all but destroyed the American Republic. This was heresy to the neoconservatives in the Reagan coalition, who put forth William J. Bennett as the anti-Bradford. Bennett was an undistinguished academic and a Democrat without conservative credentials, which made him the obvious favorite of liberal Democrats, moderate Republicans, and the media. In the end, Bennett got the job.[2]

Traditional conservatives were surprised and embittered by the neocons' attack on Bradford over a relatively unimportant post. They increasingly resented neocon influence in the Reagan administration and angrily resisted neocon efforts to define conservatism and Americanism in ways that pushed traditionalists beyond the pale. They labeled the neocons "impostors," "interlopers," "ideological vagrants," and "undocumented aliens." They also adopted a new name for themselves—*paleoconservative*—laying claim to America's conservative heritage.

The paleo/neo rift has not gone well for leading paleos, conservative or libertarian, who labor now in outer darkness while neos run the War on Terror from secure positions in the second Bush administration, the major think tanks, and the Republican Party. But the neocons' success belies the popular appeal of paleocon principles among American conservatives. Despite his dismal showing as the Reform Party candidate for president in 2000, Patrick J. Buchanan can still write boldly paleocon books that become best-sellers. Ten years ago, he was arguably the most popular conservative spokesman in the country, Rush Limbaugh notwithstanding. Indeed, Buchanan's Neocon nemesis David Frum wrote in his 1994 book *Dead Right* that Buchanan could "vie with [*Wall Street Journal* editorial-page editor] Robert Bartley and Rush Limbaugh for the title of most influential conservative in the country."[3] Were it not for 9–11, Buchanan might still be on top.

Here, *Paleoconservative* (uppercase) applies to many people not caught up in the ideological in-fighting of the Reagan years. They are descendants of the "Taft wing" of the Republican Party, heirs of the late Senator Robert A. Taft of Ohio, enemy of the New Deal, friend of America First, Midwest rival of the East Coast's Thomas Dewey, and reluctant Cold Warrior. Since Taft's death in 1953, they have devised new defenses of their older America, grounded in Christian civilization, Old Right constitutionalism, and the Anglo-American tradition of local and therefore limited government. They are the most self-consciously conservative and truly traditional of our eight options, counting Edmund Burke among their intellectual forefathers, as well as the Southern Agrarians of the inter-war years and the "New Humanists" Irving Babbitt and Paul Elmer More—two old-school scholars derided as reactionary by trendy contemporaries from H.L. Mencken to Ernest Hemingway.

Today's Paleocons are more likely to be historically minded Protestant, Catholic, or Orthodox Christians than anti-historical Evangelicals or Charismatics. There are a handful of Jews among them, mostly converts to Christianity. There are also other non-Christians whose conservatism is more racial, ethnic, and/or classical—"Anglo-Saxon-Celtic" culture with or without Greco-Roman intellectual roots. Whatever their religion, Paleocons share a respect for the wisdom of the ancients, for traditional cultures in general, and for Western civilization in particular. Consequently, they also share a pessimistic regard for recent revolutionary "progress," so often aimed at overthrowing tradition, patriarchy, Christianity, and the Eurocentric civilization of all those "dead white males."

Paleoconservatives are less anti-government than the Paleolibertarians and less individualistic than the Individualists, but often just as akratic as Indies, in their own archist way. Where Indies would expand the legal framework to protect preferred personal liberties, Paleocons would resist the elevation and centralization of power and its imperialistic expansion overseas. Where Indies would secure the blessings of liberty by binding big government to enforcing individual rights, Paleocons would secure the same blessings by keeping government local and personal, while allowing it greater discretion to guard against disruptive influences that might make individuals and communities unsuitable for self-government. The underlying assumption, in Greek philosophy and Christian tradition, is that freedom is good and we should have much of it, but man is sinful and sometimes requires restraint, less restraint when we can govern ourselves, more when we can't.

The Paleocon's liberal conservatism (as opposed to the Paleolib's conservative liberalism) is easily seen in the early thinking of the arch-traditionalist and Paleocon exemplar Russell Kirk. George Nash writes in his history of American conservatism since 1945:

Kirk's wartime letters showed the persistence of his libertarian convictions; his correspondence was replete with disgust at conscription, military inefficiency, governmental bureaucracy, "paternalism," and socialist economies. He denounced liberal "globaloney" and feared that America was doomed to live in a collectivist economy.[4]

By "libertarian convictions," Nash means Kirk's anti-statist disposition. Kirk saw the military draft as "slavery." He deplored the internment of Japanese-Americans during World War II. He opposed American involvement in the war and was convinced that Roosevelt had schemed to bring it about. In protest, he voted for the Socialist Party's Norman Thomas for president in 1944.[5]

But it wasn't just government that Kirk was against. He feared large, powerful organizations of nearly all kinds. Nash writes, "Even before his experiences at the Ford company, Kirk had developed a distaste for big business, big labor, and big government. Unions, he told a friend, were often 'more restrictive and selfish than the soulless corporations.' " Kirk sided with the corporations against the unions and the trustbusters against the corporations. Monopolies and uniformity were bad; tradition and "proliferating variety" were good. Public education was wrong in every way.[6]

As a young man, Kirk advanced what he called "Jeffersonian principles":

We must have slow but democratic decision, sound local government, diffusion of property-owning, taxation as direct as possible, preservation of civil liberties, payment of debts by the generation incurring them, prevention of the rise of class antipathies, a stable and extensive agriculture, as little governing by the government as practicable, and, above all, stimulation of self-reliance.[7]

In time, Kirk would see greater distance between Jefferson's progressivism and his own growing traditionalism, but his position would not change. His early thought already echoed the favorite themes of the upper right's ancestors: the constitutionalism of Sir Edward Coke, with its common-law limits on sovereignty; the republicanism of James Harrington, with its constitutional limits on standing armies and the size of landholdings; the semi-republicanism of Bolingbroke, with its "balance of powers" to check plutocratic interests; and the Americanism of those founding fathers whose political ideal was a free and independent republic of small towns and yeoman farmers. The common concerns are the danger of concentrations of power and wealth, a preference for limited and local government, the importance of virtue to free peoples, the sufficiency of traditional life, a distrust of progress by design, and the need to preserve accustomed liberties against an expansive, progressive government. As Kirk would write, "The cardinal principle of conservative thought is the conviction that new systems and structures incline dangerously toward presumption."[8]

Many Paleolibertarians share these concerns, but Paleocons and Paleolibs part company on what to do about them. Whereas Indies and Paleolibs agree on the libertarian means but not on the civilizational ends, Paleocons and Paleolibs agree on the civilizational ends but not on the libertarian means. To guard against abuses of wealth, dependence on foreign powers, and the corrupting influence of commercialism, Paleocons seek bounds to the marketplace that keep the "soulless corporations" honest; protect American jobs, industries, resources, and interests; check the "financialization" of the national and international economy; discourage the "dollarization" of social intimacies such as childcare and sexuality; and regulate traffic in various vices.

This hardly makes Paleocons socialists, however. Unlike Theocons and Neocons, Paleocons have never conceded defeat on the New Deal, much less the Great Society. They believe in the free market, but not always in the real-world market, in which governments everywhere are inclined to interfere. They condemn as "Wall Street socialism" the collusion of Big Government and Big Money, which they suspect has turned free trade and free markets into a rigged system protecting only the wealthiest. Their favorite Austrian School economist is Wilhelm Röpke, the Christian "localist" whose ideas guided Germany's postwar recovery and who believed that market economies depend on non-market institutions like church, family, and community, which suffer when the only aim is biggering the economy to achieve greater economies of scale.[9] Roman Catholic Paleocons often incline toward the "distributism" of Hilaire Belloc and G.K. Chesterton, which prefers cottage industry to mass production and widespread ownership of freehold property to capitalism's tendency toward concentration and indebtedness.[10]

Paleocons cannot believe in absolute economic freedom because making money is not their summum bonum. Neither is individual liberty, which is why Paleocons reject the moral subjectivism of other Austrians like Ludwig von Mises and F.A. Hayek. Paleocons agree instead with another Austrian, Joseph Schumpeter, that the stock market is a poor substitute for the Holy Grail. They agree also with Kirk that conservatism must be "something more than mere solicitude for tidy incomes." The braver among them will even agree with Chilton Williamson that "five or six centuries of industrial capitalism have probably done more to destroy traditional and humane ways of life than a century and a half of militant Marxist-Leninism."[11]

To Paleocons, capitalism in both its individualist and corporatist forms is not necessarily conservative and often in fact destructively progressive. Pat Buchanan writes that "just as globalism is the antithesis of patriotism, the transnational corporation is the natural antagonist of tradition." Clyde Wilson, a Southern partisan and authority on John C. Calhoun, writes, "The hardest tasks for conservatives will be to convince our capitalist allies that the common rights of humanity, as embodied in the family, and our civil rights as Englishmen and Americans take precedence over our desire for profits and productivity."[12]

This concern for things other than profits and productivity has often pitted the Paleocons in the upper right against the plutocratic establishment in the lower right, sometimes in ways that make the Paleocons look downright progressive.

Consider the case of Hamilton Fish III, scion of a well-to-do and politically active Hudson Valley Republican family and an even better example of Richard Hofstadter's "conservative progressivism" than Teddy Roosevelt.[13] Fish's great-grandfather was an aide to Alexander Hamilton in the Revolutionary War and later a staunch Federalist. His grandfather, Hamilton Fish I, was governor of New York, a United States senator, and President Grant's secretary of state. His father was a congressman and assistant U.S. treasurer under President William Howard Taft. But Fish himself began his political career as a "Bull Moose" Progressive, bucking the GOP establishment to back Theodore Roosevelt's independent run for the White House in 1912. Two years later, Fish was elected to the state assembly on a fusion ticket of Democrats and Progressives.

In Fish's early years, more than ever, the Republican Party stood for the dominant business interests of the Gilded Age; the Democratic Party represented a broad range of resistance to that power, including bitter Southerners, struggling farmers, recent immigrants, and social reformers. The Progressives were a nationalist strain of populist resistance to the business establishment. Men like Fish were inspired by Teddy Roosevelt to see their duty as looking out for all Americans and protecting the Republic from the big bosses of business, politics, and labor whose aims were more selfish. Thus they supported trustbusting and other reforms to bring the business world under the rule of law, guarantee every American a "square deal," defend common American interests at home and abroad, and conserve national treasures.[14]

It wasn't until Franklin Roosevelt's first term that the latent conservatism of many Progressive Republicans began to appear. By then a veteran congressman, Fish supported some of FDR's early reforms, including the minimum wage and Social Security, but he soon became an outspoken enemy of the New Deal, one of three leading obstructionists in the House whom FDR mocked in a 1940 speech with the refrain "Martin, Barton, and

Fish." Fish also thought FDR was too soft on the Soviets and opposed FDR's efforts on their behalf, later accusing FDR of maneuvering the United States into World War II by forcing Japan's hand.[15]

Fish backed his friend and ally Senator Robert A. Taft over New York Governor Thomas E. Dewey in 1940. In return, Dewey gerrymandered Fish out of Congress in 1944. He never again held office, but he continued speaking out for the next four decades against FDR, the New Deal, communism, Thomas Dewey, the "business wing" of the Republican Party, President Eisenhower's security guarantees to Southeast Asia, the Vietnam War, atheists, secular humanists, the "one-worlders" of the Trilateralist Commission, nuclear weapons, and the arms race. He supported the invasions of Grenada in 1983 and Panama in 1989, still believing in the Monroe Doctrine, but he was ambivalent about the Gulf War, in which he did not see a clear American interest. Before he died in 1991, at the age of 102, he confessed that he admired just two American presidents: Teddy Roosevelt and Ronald Reagan, in that order.

Similar sentiments are seen more recently in conservatives such as the Paleocon Boadicea, Phyllis Schlafly. A native of St. Louis, Schlafly fits easily within the Taftian tradition of Midwestern conservatism, with its emphasis on local government, individual self-reliance, traditional American values, and strictly defined national interests. In 1964, Schlafly wrote *A Choice Not an Echo* touting Barry Goldwater for president. Before organizing the "Stop ERA" movement in the 1970s, Schlafly's main interest was foreign policy. She still writes often on foreign policy, in defense of American sovereignty and against military intervention in places like the Balkans. Opposition to the Equal Rights Amendment (ERA) came naturally to Schlafly, as to all Paleocons, because the ERA would have used *kratos* to destroy a traditional *archê*. By definition, Paleocons are mostly for *archê* and mostly against *kratos*.

The best-known Paleocon today is still Pat Buchanan, a latter-day Bolingbroke still brandishing the banner of an ancient constitution against triumphant Whig commercialism. Buchanan frankly prefers an older America—before the Immigration Act of 1965, before the Sexual Revolution, before the corruption of the American imagination by the "cultural Marxists" of the Frankfurt School, before "compulsive interventionism" and "free-trade-*über-alles*" captured the hearts and minds of the Republican Party. He is an American nationalist for whom "the nation" means a specific people sharing a common cultural heritage, not an artificial association of strangers under contract to a vague set of universal principles— liberty, equality, diversity, prosperity, progress, democracy, capitalism, etc.

Among Paleocons, Buchanan is a moderate with populist tendencies. He rejects the "isolationist" label, but proudly confesses himself a protectionist.

As a candidate, he made much of the need to protect American jobs and industries. He is also solidly pro-life, backing a human-life amendment and the reversal of *Roe v. Wade.* On most other issues, he has taken moderate stands. He is for parental choice in education, but not against public schools or public funding of private schools through vouchers. He is against affirmative action, but not anti-discrimination laws, which most Paleolibs would repeal. Buchanan would "end illegal immigration" but allow legal immigration at "manageable levels." He would reduce government spending and regulation, but use the tax code and other government policies to favor marriage and the family. He would not expand NATO, but not pull out of it. He would cut taxes in various ways and consider alternatives to the current tax system, but he stops short of endorsing more radical reforms and opposes the flat tax as anti-family.[16]

Such stands hardly put Buchanan outside the Republican mainstream, although they do distance him from the GOP leadership, which always treads lightly on social issues (e.g., abortion, affirmative action, immigration) and inclines toward a more hawkish stance on foreign affairs. In 1999, Buchanan and Alan Keyes were the only Republican presidential hopefuls to oppose bombing Serbia over Kosovo. John McCain, Steve Forbes, and Elizabeth Dole boldly backed bombing; Gary Bauer and George W. Bush were less gung-ho but not opposed. In Congress, however, Republicans acted overwhelmingly as Buchananites: 86 percent in the House and 70 percent in the Senate voted against bombing. Republicans in Congress also voted against sending troops to Bosnia in 1995.

Rank-and-file Republicans also join Buchanan in opposing open borders and supporting a crackdown on illegal aliens. Paleocons in general are the only camp unequivocally opposed to high levels of legal and illegal immigration, and polls regularly show about two thirds of all voters and three fourths to four fifths of Republican voters likewise opposed. The House regularly votes to toughen enforcement at the border, though the Senate and the Bush administration have regularly blocked enforcement and pushed for opening the border to even more immigrants.

Even trade does not set Buchanan apart from the GOP. The party leadership talks a good line on free trade, but the Republican record in Congress and the White House is mixed, favoring fast-track free-trade deals but also steel quotas and farm subsidies, even while pushing policy toward more free trade.

For a Paleocon platform clearly outside the Republican mainstream, we must turn to the Constitution Party, founded in 1992 as the U.S. Taxpayers Party, whose presidential candidate for many years was Howard Phillips, chairman of the Conservative Caucus and President Reagan's director of the Office of Economic Opportunity. The U.S. Taxpayers Party had a quasi-libertarian beginning. Among its founders was Ron Paul, Libertarian Party candidate for president in 1988 and now a Republican congressman. The party promised to "roll back the clock 30 years on taxes, on spending, and on regulation" and to "roll it back 200 years" on constitutional interpretation. "In plain English," Phillips wrote in 1992, "if it's not in the Constitution, then neither our politicians, our bureaucrats, not even our judges, can lawfully take our money or regulate our activities."[17]

Since then, under the influence of the late Protestant theologian R.J. Rushdoony, the party has become more overtly Christian. Its original platform acknowledged the "blessing of the Lord God as Creator, Preserver and Ruler of the Universe and of this Nation." Its 2000 platform adds a declaration of "our full submission and unshakable faith in our Savior and Redeemer, our Lord Jesus Christ." But the dominant theme of the platform is still a super-strict constitutionalism, based on natural, inalienable rights to "Life, Liberty, Property and the Pursuit of the individual's personal interest" and the need to "bind government with the chains of the Constitution and carefully divide and jealously limit government powers to those assigned by the consent of the governed."[18]

The Constitution Party would therefore eliminate most of what is now the federal government. It would revive the Tenth Amendment reserving to the States and the people all powers not expressly delegated to the federal government; repeal the Seventh Amendment to again allow state governments to choose senators; abolish congressional salaries and pensions and restore the use of per diem allowances; return to the gold standard and repeal the Federal Reserve Act; replace the current tax system with revenue tariffs and state levies; make participation in the Social Security system optional; end federal involvement in education, welfare, environmental, and safety regulation; institute a moratorium on immigration; make English the official language and a precondition of citizenship; provide a strong national defense; and adopt an America-first foreign policy. The party would pull out of NATO and the United Nations, stop all foreign aid, and withdraw U.S. support for virtually all international organizations. "We should be the friend of liberty everywhere, but the guarantor and provisioner of ours alone," the platform declares, with many more words against the New World Order that echo John Adams's last words to the American people: "Independence forever!"

There is not much in the Constitution Party's platform that most Paleoconservatives would disagree with, but there is also not much in it that most Paleocons still believe can come to pass. Many more populist Paleocons are still in the political game, carrying on the fight against the progressive Left while yet complaining about the sacrifice of civil liberties in the War on Terror and the worship of wealth and power by the Republican establishment. But the success of other conservatives has forced some erstwhile Paleocons to migrate elsewhere. Kevin Phillips left the upper right long ago and no longer calls himself any kind of conservative. In an article entitled "Why I Am No Longer a Conservative," in the inaugural issue of *The American Conservative*, he wrote:

Much ideological water has flowed under the bridge since I began writing *The Emerging Republican Majority* in the wake of the 1966 midterm elections. In recent years, I have come to believe that "conservatism"—broadly defined as the shared politics, policy, and practice of the Republican-led House of Representatives and the Bush White House—has become an arrogant defender of ideological excess and entrenched interests and privileges. . . .

At some risk of oversimplification, the power structure Washington conservatism now represents can be described as Wall Street, Big Energy, multinational corporations, the Military-Industrial Complex, the Religious Right, the Market Extremist think-tanks, and the Rush Limbaugh Axis.[19]

Once a prophet of the Right's resurgence, Phillips decries the dominance of "market Darwinism" within the Republican Party, likening it to the "social Darwinism" of the Gilded Age. He now espouses an anti-Republican populism whose main complaint is the concentration of wealth and power in the hands of a few.[20]

More ideologically sophisticated Paleocons know they have lost not just the political battle, but the culture war as well. "In half a lifetime, many Americans have seen their God dethroned, their heroes defiled, their culture polluted, their values assaulted, their country invaded, and themselves demonized as extremists and bigots for holding on to beliefs Americans have held for generations," writes Pat Buchanan in *The Death of the West*. "America has undergone a cultural and social revolution. We are not the same country that we were in 1970 or even 1980. We are not the same people."[21]

Like the sad survivors of *King Lear*, their present business is general woe, and many Paleocons are now inclined to take Edgar's advice at the play's *exeunt*: "The weight of this sad time we must obey, Speak what we feel, not what we ought to say." So they concentrate their efforts not on politics, but on continuing their cultural critique of the past and the present, deliberately disrespecting the sacred cows of modern culture, while preserving as best they can the culture bequeathed to them, saving it up for the morrow, if only in microcosm. Long ago, in fact, the Catholic traditionalist Frederick Wilhelmsen lamented, "We conservatives have lost our kings and our chivalry.... We have nothing to offer the world but our vision."[22]

For those high up in the upper right, this has meant a shift in emphasis from specifically American traditions and to what Russell Kirk called "the permanent things," evident in the longer European experience with Christian civilization. The early American ideal they now think irredeemably lost beneath the waves of Third World immigration and militant multiculturalism. Reflecting on the situation twenty years ago, at the founding of *Chronicles* magazine, Thomas Fleming, now president of the Rockford Institute, wrote, "The agrarian republic of Washington and Jefferson had been overthrown by Lincoln and replaced by an imperial republic, which was in turn replaced by the warm-and-fuzzy national socialism imposed by FDR." He continued:

We never thought we could restore the authentic Old Republic or even the Imperial Republic, but we did believe that, just as our grandparents and parents managed to salvage some good things out the shipwreck of American traditions, we could do the same, and even though the political battle over immigration has been lost—as any battle will be when the socialist left of the New Republic joins the capitalist left of the Wall Street Journal—there are many options open to Americans, although none of them are political.[23]

At perhaps a more exuberant moment, Fleming declares, "We must work toward the recreation of Christendom in North America and Europe."[24]

It follows that Paleoconservatives are natural enemies of all who seek to diversify, secularize, and de-Christianize American society. It follows also that they are not natural allies of Israel or of any other foreign country that lobbies for an interventionist United States for the sake of its own security. They are defensive and not expansive nationalists. Their nationalism stresses independence, national sovereignty, cultural particularism, and minding your own business among nations. This conflicts with the Neocons' nationalism, which stresses global security, American dominance, the universality of American values, and a with-us-or-against-us approach to international relations.

As fans of the nation-state, Paleocons were once quite sympathetic to Jewish nationalism and Zionism in particular. In the 1920s, Hamilton Fish sponsored a House resolution endorsing a Jewish homeland in Palestine, the American equivalent of Britain's Balfour Declaration. During the Cold War, Paleocons like Pat Buchanan strongly supported Israel as part of the anti-Soviet alliance. But Paleocons have always viewed America as a Christian nation, and since the end of the Cold War they have protested the sacrifice of Christian and American interests to Jewish and Israeli interests. This has brought them charges of antisemitism, most notably against Thomas Fleming, Patrick Buchanan, Joseph Sobran, and even Russell Kirk, who once remarked in a speech at the Heritage Foundation that "not seldom has it seemed as if some eminent neoconservatives mistook Tel Aviv for the capital of the United States."[25]

Sobran has taken the most heat and shown the most defiance. Since breaking with his former friend and mentor William F. Buckley Jr., Sobran has started his own newsletter, written a book on Shakespeare and a book on the abandonment of the Constitution, and run for vice president as Howard Phillips's running mate. He hovers now in the akratic ether of the upper right, penning Chestertonian attacks on the progressive cultural establishment he calls "the Hive" and more conventional critiques of the State borrowed from his Paleolib compadres. But if he shares the Paleolibs' antipathy toward the State, he hasn't quite figured out how to square his anarchist temptation with his Roman Catholicism. He concedes that the Church has always taught that the State is at least a necessary evil on account of Original Sin. "But we may ask whether this is really so," he writes. "Whatever the truth is, the anarchists have much reason on their side. And much history."[26]

But we may ask whether this is really so, and whether Sobran's archic akratism is not the right-wing reverse of Gore Vidal's akratic anarchism. Both Sobran and Vidal warm to the anti-statist revolt of Lew Rockwell's Rothbardian Paleolibs, but both also retain strong ties to the Right and Left, respectively, and neither is quite convincing as a Rothbardian "anarcho-capitalist" eager to submit every choice to the ultimate arbiter of value, the Almighty Market.

The sympathy the three feel at the moment is more likely to be a demonstration of the common phenomenon of agreeing extremes: When any corner of the Compass enjoys too much success, the extremes in the other three corners gang up against him. In this case, the Neocon crusade known as the War on Terror has provoked an intense anti-Neocon response making bedfellows of Joe Sobran, Lew Rockwell, Gore Vidal, Noam Chomsky, and Michael Lerner.

Chapter 9

God and Country: The Theoconservative

I know not what to make of a republic of thirty million atheists.
John Adams

Economics, politics, and social policy are by no means the most important questions in life. But they are important. To the extent that Christians think about them, they should want to think about them Christianly.
Richard John Neuhaus
Doing Well & Doing Good

Cal Thomas voted for Jimmy Carter in 1976. Thomas had recently become a committed Christian, and Carter seemed a "serious churchman, a moral man and a breath of fresh air" in the aftermath of Watergate. But Thomas felt the air turn foul as the Carter administration took shape. "While I continued to regard him as personally upright," Thomas writes, "I increasingly felt there was a gap between what Scripture taught—about unborn human life, especially—and Carter's political stand."[1]

Before Carter was out of the White House, Thomas had jumped the fence between journalism and politics to become the spokesman for the Moral Majority, a new coalition of religious conservatives headed by Baptist minister Jerry Falwell. For five years, Thomas was Falwell's Jeremiah, warning Washington of the wrath to come if America turned away God. The Moral Majority's early success in helping to elect Ronald Reagan in 1980 raised high hopes for returning the country to the true path, but in time the disappointments and compromises mounted and other players crowded in.

Thomas soured not on politics, but on Christian activism. He returned to journalism as a syndicated columnist and was soon directing jeremiads at other Christians whom he judged guilty of mixing politics and religion.

So it went for the Religious Right in general: a late start in politics, early overconfidence on account of their belief that God was on their side, difficulty sorting out the political and theological details, repeated disappointments leading to disenchantment with the dream and a return to the things that matter most—faith and family. Part of their problem is ancient and enduring: There is an unavoidable tension between religion and politics wherever and whenever the religion is Christianity. But today's Christians have the added difficulty of bearing witness democratically without overstepping the divine division of labor between church and state. They must also struggle against forces still pressing for the complete eradication of the vestigial Christian order in which the two partners of church and state cooperate.

Until the 1960s, the Christian order did not appear to many American Christians to be politically threatened. There was the threat of "godless Communism," but that had been suppressed at home and contained overseas. The home-grown socialism of the New Deal and public schooling was an accepted part of American life in the early Cold War and not so obviously anti-Christian. With nothing to unite them politically, conservative Christians were scattered in all directions by sect, class, ethnicity, and region and did not appear as a distinct perspective.

Then came the social upheavals of the 1960s and 1970s, in which government was not neutral. The Supreme Court banished prayer and scripture from public schools, extended constitutional protection to pornography, and invalidated state laws against abortion. Congress began making feminism the law of land with the Equal Pay Act of 1963, the Civil Rights Act of 1964, the Education Act's Title IX in 1972, the Equal Employment Opportunity Act of 1972, the Equal Rights Amendment (ERA) in 1972, and the forced integration of the federal service academies in 1975. Public schools replaced religious reverence with secular humanism, taught evolution as scientific fact, added sex education to the curriculum, and stopped making distinctions between boys and girls. Around the country, laws against contraception, fornication, sodomy, pornography, obscenity, and gambling fell by the wayside. With them went the "blue laws" keeping stores closed on Sunday, a feature of Christian civilization since the early fourth century.

Many of these changes meant less use of government coercion, but many also meant more. To conservative Christians, government had simply switched sides. The American people remained overwhelmingly

Christian, but their government had turned atheistic, anti-religious, and Christophobic. The country suffered under an "unelected oligarchy" of Supreme Court justices overruling the democratic wishes of the American people (Pat Robertson). "Religious apartheid" denied people of faith full participation in public institutions (Cal Thomas). The result was a "naked public square" in which religion was no longer welcome (Richard John Neuhaus).

The response was the creation of organizations like the Moral Majority, Concerned Women for America, the American Family Association, the Christian Coalition, and the Human Life League. Many of the people behind these groups had been Democrats before the 1970s. Many also were entering politics for the first time. From the start, their interests were more moral than political, and more social than economic. Their first and last concern was the preservation of the Christian *archê*, a social order founded upon religious faith and family life. On the political use of *kratos*, they were ambivalent, for or against the force of government depending upon its effect on faith and family.

Still sometimes called the Christian Right, the Religious Right, or, less specifically, social conservatives, they are today more and more called *theoconservatives*. Not all theoconservatives are Christian. Not all are even religious. But all see society and politics in mainly moral terms. They are moralists even more than they are theoconservatives. They believe in a universal moral authority to which all are subject, exercised in society mainly by families and religious institutions. Their political thinking focuses on the application of this moral authority to the operation of the state, a matter of both warrants and limits. This contrasts with the Paleocons' focus on the cultural traditions of particular historical communities and with the Neocons' focus on dominant political and economic interests.

At first the Theoconservatives' goals were nothing less than the reversal of recent losses: overturning *Roe v. Wade*, returning prayer to public schools, banning pornography, reinstating curbs on various vices, and stopping ratification of the ERA. Many still saw America as a Christian nation. They accepted the separation of church and state, but felt that the Supreme Court had recently raised the "wall of separation" too high. In a speech to the Yale University Law School in 1986, Pat Robertson argued that the First Amendment applied only to Congress, not to school boards, city councils, or state legislatures. Religion, he said, was a necessary support to morality: "If you don't have some form of religion, you're not going to have public morality. But the court has stripped us of the ability to muster this morality."[2] Later that year, announcing his run for president in 1988, Robertson declared, "There can be no education without morality, and there can be no lasting morality without religion. For the sake of our children, we must bring God back to the classrooms of America!"[3]

Today the Theocons' big issues are abortion, gay marriage, the Pledge of Allegiance, pornography, parental rights, family-friendly taxes, freedom of religious expression, and judicial mischief. On each, they seek from government a mix of freedom and favor—freedom from government control of religious life and child-rearing, favor in the form of curbs on immorality and cooperation with families and religious groups. On education, for example, Theocons push a variety of reforms aimed at freeing education from government control (deregulation of private and home schools, tuition vouchers or tax credits) while still using government schools to teach traditional values (local and parental control of public schools, strict discipline, dress codes, abstinence education, student-led prayer, the teaching of creation alongside evolution). Others fault them for inconsistency on these two approaches, but both approaches are entirely consistent with the Theocons' objective of wresting education away from the progressive education establishment.

At a lower level of commitment and interest to Theocons are economic issues like taxes, government spending, regulation, and trade. Theocons have taken up these issues in part out of sincere belief in private enterprise, but also in part to be good team players in the Republican Party. They really are "pro-life, pro-family, pro-growth"—the motto of Gary Bauer's Campaign for Working Families. But there are good reasons why growth ranks third—indeed a distant third—and why economics is never a motivational issue for Theocons. On one hand, Theocons accept the conservative critique of big government as a drag on prosperity and generally regard the corporate world or the free market with favor. On the other hand, Theocons see greed, materialism, and selfishness as sins and do not believe the country's many problems can be solved by material means, whether economic growth or government aid. Compared to other conservatives, Theocons are neither as pro-market as Paleolibs, nor as pro-business as Neocons. In their basic beliefs, Theocons do not see society as an open market of individuals freely interacting through exchanges of value. Rather, they see society as an assembly of closely knit groups held together by common values and interests, as well as faith and love.

Conservative Christians were not always so favorably disposed toward capitalism. Until the mid-twentieth century, consciously Christian Americans were more likely to view big business with suspicion. Southerners hated Yankees. Farmers feared bankers. Catholics resented the WASP elite. The serious Christian could not help but contrast Christian charity with the "social Darwinism" of the Gilded Age. It was an article of faith that God was on the side of the poor and humble, and not the rich and proud. Christian economic sensibilities contributed to the Populist movement of the late nineteenth century, whose leaders like William Jennings Bryan were more preachers than politicians, and whose rallies assumed the aspect of revivals.[4]

In the twentieth century, however, the Communist threat forced conservative Christians to rethink their economic assumptions. Catholic intellectuals such as Edward Keller, John Dinneen, John T. Noonan Jr., and later Michael Novak developed detailed rationales for Christian capitalism, which were then popularized by William F. Buckley's *National Review* and adopted by the later generations of conservative Catholics.[5] Conservative Protestants needed less convincing on account of their already individualistic Anglo-Saxon heritage, but the defense of capitalism mounted by Catholic intellectuals help to solidify the thinking on the Christian right, making both Catholic and Protestant Theoconservatives better fits for the Republican Party.

And yet, on economics, Theoconservatives still bear some similarity to their opposites, the Radicals. Both are social and communal in their outlook. Both are also morally idealistic. They differ, though, in their conceptions of community and in their moral ideals. Radicals trust only anarchical groups governed by leaderless consensus; Theocons trust archical groups like families, churches, companies, and nations, which all have their heads. Radicals are revolutionary, wanting to throw off their masters; Theocons are conservative, believing in the necessity of authority and discipline. Radicals seek justice in this world; Theocons seek salvation in the next.

Despite their communal outlook, Theocons as a group are ambivalent toward government aid to the needy, inclined neither to surrender all social work to government, nor to oppose all of government aid on principle. Few Theocons believe that government should do nothing to help the needy. "Private property is not entirely private," writes Richard John Neuhaus in *Doing Well & Doing Good: The Challenge to the Christian Capitalist.* "That is, it is not something to be grasped entirely for itself, or for oneself. Ownership can be *legally* free and clear, but it is not *morally* free and clear."[6] At the same time, many Theocons believe that personal hardships are often self-inflicted and that public welfare often subsidizes misbehavior. "The answer for us does not lie in institutionalizing aberrant behavior," Pat Robertson declared at his 1986 campaign kickoff. "And certainly the answer does not lie in once again penalizing the productive sector of our society with high taxes and wasteful spending."[7]

This difference is partly religious. Evangelicals like Robertson are closer to the Anglo-Saxon tradition of limited government, individualistic religion, and the vaunted Protestant work ethic. Lutherans and Catholics like Neuhaus (a Lutheran who turned Catholic) have inherited the Continental tradition of church and state working together to care for the sick and the poor.

But the difference is also evidence of the dilemma Christians always face when asking the state for both freedom and favor. Christians themselves are divided on whether both can be had safely. Some seek government assistance for "faith-based" social work. Others fear that taking the king's shilling will cost them their independence.

The hope of assistance is behind the "compassionate conservatism" urged on George W. Bush by Marvin Olasky, a professor of journalism at the University of Texas at Austin and the editor of *World* magazine, an Evangelical equivalent of *Time*. Olasky's 1992 book *The Tragedy of American Compassion* chronicled the displacement of successful, private, faith-based welfare programs of the late nineteenth century by less successful, public, secular welfare programs of the twentieth century. Olasky briefed Bush on the book and his version of "compassionate conservatism" in 1993, when Bush was preparing to run for governor of Texas. Later as governor, Bush contributed a foreword to Olasky's *Compassionate Conservatism*, published in 2000.

Olasky's compassionate conservatism is based on the belief that poverty is a "spiritual as well as a material problem: most poor people don't have the faith that they and their situations can change." Government in a pluralistic society can't give them faith, but it can fund the faith-based efforts of others. Olasky rejects the argument that a "wall of separation" bars government from doing so, citing the early efforts by founding fathers Patrick Henry and Joseph Story to provide public support to churches for education and welfare. The only requirement should be that government not take sides among the faiths. "Compassionate conservatives know that in a pluralistic society, 'faith-based' cannot be code for 'Christian,'" he writes. "It's time to have a new attitude based on the decision to promote diversity not by banning religion, but by encouraging many beliefs to compete."[8]

Many Theocons might nod in agreement that that's how things should work, but many also would second Robert Bork's reservations about government aid in his 1996 book *Slouching Towards Gomorrah*:

A few necessary actions must involve the government, as in capturing and punishing criminals, and, perhaps, in administering censorship of the vilest aspects of our popular culture; otherwise, government must be kept at a distance. When, for example, black churches try to save the youth of the inner city, the financial and moral support for that effort must be private. Government is largely responsible for making the inner cities what they are. Perhaps government can stop doing harm by reforming welfare, but it should leave to private institutions the task of redeeming the culture.[9]

Here, Bork offers an even older Christian view of government, a wary pre-Constantinian view, according to which the state is ordained by God to restrain evil, but is otherwise unsafe. The Christian warrant for government is based on the Apostle Paul's warning to the Romans:

Let every soul be subject unto the higher powers. For there is no power but of God: the powers that be are ordained of God. Whosoever therefore resisteth the power, resisteth the ordinance of God: and they that resist shall receive to themselves damnation. For rulers are not a terror to good works, but to the evil. . . . For he is a minister of God to thee for good. But if thou do that which is evil, be afraid; for he beareth not the sword in vain: for he is the minister of God, a revenger to execute wrath upon him that doeth evil. (Romans 13:1–4)

The Christian wariness toward government owes more to the recurring persecutions of Christians by Roman authorities. It reappears today because Theocons again feel themselves persecuted by anti-Christian authorities. Bork points an accusing finger at the anarchistic corners of our Compass, the upper left and the lower left, on which he blames the "twin thrusts of modern liberalism: radical individualism and radical egalitarianism." Together these extreme anarchisms form a revolutionary tyranny that permits what it should persecute and persecutes what it should permit, destroying the free and independent social order in the process:

Radical egalitarianism necessarily presses us towards collectivism because a powerful state is required to suppress the difference that freedom produces. That raises the sinister and seemingly paradoxical possibility that radical individualism is the handmaiden of collectivist tyranny. This individualism, it is quite apparent in our time, attacks the authority of family, church, and private association. The family is said to be oppressive, the fount of our miseries. It is denied that the church may legitimately insist upon what it regards as moral behavior in its members. Private associations are routinely denied the autonomy to define their membership for themselves. The upshot is that these institutions, which stand between the state and the individual, are progressively weakened and their functions increasingly dictated or taken over by the state. The individual becomes less of a member of powerful private institutions and more a member of an unstructured mass that is vulnerable to the collectivist coercion of the state.[10]

Just how these twin demons arose, Bork does not say. "The wonder is that the culture of liberalism triumphed over conventional middle-class culture so rapidly," he writes. After all, liberty and equality "produced the great political, social, and cultural achievements of Western civilization." The twentieth century, he thinks, just carried them too far.[11]

This historical short-sightedness is typical of Theocons. Pat Robertson will go back as far as the eighteenth-century Illuminati in tracing the anti-Christian origins of the modern Left, but most Theocons very much want to believe that America was on the right track until very recently. Theocons tend to see America as a light unto the gentiles, a God-favored nation whose founding was providential. They typically lay great stress on the Christian faith of the founding fathers and interpret the Declaration of the Independence and the Constitution (as Neuhaus would say) *Christianly*. Alan Keyes, as always, leaves no doubt where he stands:

We've had people who call themselves conservatives in America who want to throw out the Declaration because they claim it's some kind of deistic, naturalistic document that rejects religion. I beg to differ. I believe that it is absolutely clear, in everything the Founders did, that they intended the Declaration to be a bridge between the Bible and the Constitution, between the basis of our moral faith and the basis of our political life.[12]

Compared to the historically minded and more traditional Paleocons, the morally minded Theocons are downright progressive. Protestant Theocons see steady progress since the Reformation. Catholic Theocons assume a gradual development of Christian civilization. Neither places primary emphasis on tradition as a source of authority. Protestants have long viewed tradition as a burden to avoid. Catholics have subordinated tradition to reason and Rome. Both have used reinterpretations of scripture and reformulations of theology to move with the times. Both see the political issues of our day in terms of right and wrong, not old and new. Neuhaus, for example, describes himself as "religiously orthodox, culturally conservative, politically liberal, and economically pragmatic." But being "orthodox" and even "conservative" is not the same thing as being "traditional," a word Neuhaus does not apply to himself, and by "politically liberal," Neuhaus means tolerant, pluralistic, and progressive like "what today is called neoconservatism."[13]

For a Protestant example, consider Ralph Reed, former executive director of the Christian Coalition, who went to great lengths to assure Americans that the Religious Right did not want to turn back the clock:

Religious conservatives want to move forward, not backward. They believe that many of the social advances of the past thirty years can and must be acknowledged and preserved. For example, the movement of women to a position of equality in the workplace where they can advance as far as their talents can carry them is clearly progress. . . . Those who suggest that people of faith look nostalgically back to the 1950s and Ozzie and Harriet are mistaken.[14]

Here, the very politically minded Reed, as always, leans toward the Neocon position and overstates his disclaimer, but he could not get away with it in his own crowd if it were not true of many Theocons. In fact, hardly any Theocons still adhere to the biblical and patristic teaching on the silence, veiling, and subjection of women, though that teaching was still broadly accepted by American Christians as late as the benighted 1950s. Today most Theocons raise their girls much like their boys, in co-ed schools that emphasize sports and careers for both equally. They complain about radical feminism, but they could not be mobilized against the feminization of the American military. The Christian Right did help defeat the ERA, but that fight was led by a Paleocon, Phyllis Schlafly.

In the aftermath of the Paleocon/Neocon rift in the 1980s, the Theocons aligned themselves with the winner. Neuhaus broke abruptly with the Rockford Institute and founded *First Things*, a Christian incarnation of the American Jewish Committee's *Commentary*. Reed worked hard to align the Christian Coalition's agenda with GOP interests and make allies of leading Neocons like William J. Bennett, who wrote the foreword to Reed's 1994 book *Politically Incorrect*, which was written to make the Coalition appear as politically correct as possible. Gary Bauer, as head of Family Research Council, the political arm of James Dobson's Focus on the Family, plotted a similar course, standing firm on moral issues but taking a moderate line on economics and a hard line on foreign affairs.

The affinity of Theos and Neos made sense in many ways. Both fear the effects of liberalism on the social fabric. Both believe in free enterprise but also an active role for government. Both honor the founding fathers, American democracy, and America's immigrant identity. Both are forward-looking and accepting of most of the modern federal system, including existing civil-rights laws. Both stress universal values, in contrast to Paleocons and Paleolibs, who stress the forgotten importance of cultural particulars. Both believe in American exceptionalism, seeing the United States as playing a special messianic role in history. Both believe in a moral basis to foreign policy and in the assertive use of American power in the world. Both are big fans of Israel, albeit for different reasons. Neocons see no difference between the United States and Israel, while many Theocons see Israel as a key piece of the end-times puzzle.

But by the mid-1990s, the strains in this alliance had already begun to show. The Theocons still weren't getting what they wanted politically, from the federal courts or from Congress, even after the Republican takeover of Congress in 1994. Congress's failure to override President Clinton's veto of a ban on partial-birth abortions in 1996 brought angry complaints against the GOP establishment from leading Theocons such as Paul Weyrich, Gary Bauer, James Dobson, Charles Colson, and Richard John Neuhaus. That year, *First Things* published a symposium entitled "The End of Democracy?" on the "judicial usurpation of politics." The contributors—Robert Bork, Russell Hittinger, Hadley Arkes, Charles Colson, and Robert P. George— probed the provocative question of whether the nation might be "reaching the point where conscientious citizens can no longer give moral assent to the existing regime."[15]

Leading Neocons were appalled. Gertrude Himmelfarb and Peter Berger resigned from *First Things'* editorial board. Walter Berns quit the journal's editorial advisory board. Norman Podhoretz denounced Neuhaus for giving "aid and comfort" to the "bomb throwers among us." Himmelfarb wrote that the Theocons' question "can only confirm many Americans in their suspicion that cultural conservatism is outside the 'mainstream' of American politics." William Bennett took exception to the disrespectful characterization of American democracy as a "regime" and insisted, "We are still America, not 'Amerika.' "[16]

Other differences emerged the following year, when Neocons William Kristol and David Brooks, writing in *The Wall Street Journal*, attacked conservatives for being anti-government and put forth their vision of "national greatness conservatism." Marvin Olasky, editor of *World* magazine, responded with a column entitled "National Greatness: Looking for Purpose in All the Wrong Places." Olasky wrote that Kristol and Brooks posited a false dichotomy of selfish individualism and heroic nationalism. "Christians know there is a third alternative," Olasky wrote:

We do not build a great nation by emphasizing "national greatness." Our nation achieves greatness when ministers unselfishly serve their congregations, teachers and coaches sacrificially minister to their students, businessmen build enterprises that create good products and good jobs, and parents train their children in the way they should go. . . . For decades, Europe emphasized nationalism, but America was a land of church-based associations. In recent decades, however, government expansion has marginalized many "mediating structures," those community and religious institutions that stand between the individual and the state. The greatest political task for the next decade is to find ways to make such groups central once more.[17]

Disenchantment with politics is almost inevitable for Theocons. Deep down they just don't believe that politics matters that much. No other position around the Compass has seen as many of its leaders withdraw from active involvement in its cause. Jerry Falwell closed the Moral Majority in 1989 and has since kept a much lower political profile. Ralph Reed left the Christian Coalition in 1997 to pursue a more mainstream career within Republican Party (he had been a GOP operative before becoming a Christian activist). Pat Robertson left the Coalition in 2001 to concentrate on his broadcasting business. Robertson now styles himself a "Jeffersonian conservative by nature, who believes that government governs best that governs least. . . . I am more of a laissez-faire type of conservative in terms of what the role of government is."[18]

Paul Weyrich has all but announced to the world that the Theocons' political cause is lost, at least until conservatives can take back the culture. Weyrich has tried to focus his own efforts on defining and encouraging "cultural conservatism," but the results have looked suspiciously like paleoconservatism to Neocon critics like Gertrude Himmelfarb. A veteran activist, in at the founding of both the Moral Majority and the Heritage Foundation, Weyrich has many friends in the Old Right and has always been more traditional and more anti-government than most Theocons. He recently joined such unlikely allies as Walter Cronkite, Morton Halperin, and Abner Mikva to warn against the sacrifice of civil rights in the war on Islamic terrorism.[19]

For a while, it looked as if Theocons were on their way out of politics. In 2000, they fielded two candidates for the GOP nomination for president, Gary Bauer and Alan Keyes. When neither took off, Theocons backed George W. Bush half-heartedly. Bush talked up faith-based programs and his own personal faith, naming Jesus Christ as his inspiration, but voter turnout in the 2000 general election among white Evangelical Protestants was much lower than the Bush campaign expected. "If you look at the electoral model, there should have been 19 million of them. Instead, there was 15 million," Bush advisor Karl Rove said in December 2001. "We may have failed to mobilize them." On the other hand, said Rove, "I think we may be seeing to some degree . . . a return to the sidelines of some of these previously politically involved religious conservatives."[20]

But 9-11 did more to rally Theocons behind the Republican Party than Rove could foresee. It forged closer immediate bonds between Theocons and Neocons on the need to defend Israel and defeat Islam. It also made Theocons an indispensable support for an administration committed to a costly and controversial war. Other issues such as gay marriage, the Pledge of Allegiance, and the looming vacancies on the Supreme Court have drawn Theocons back into the fray with added ardor. Theocons are easily disappointed and won't be taken for granted, but right now they show no signs of letting up.

Chapter 10

Mugged by Reality: The Neoconservative

All communities divide themselves into the few and the many. The first are the rich and wellborn, the other the mass of the people.... The people are turbulent and changing; they seldom judge or determine right. Give therefore to the first class a distinct, permanent share in the government. They will check the unsteadiness of the second, and as they cannot receive any advantage by a change, they therefore will ever maintain good government.

Alexander Hamilton, 1787

In the last couple of weeks, there's been too much pseudo-populism, almost too much concern and attention for, quote, the people.... After all, we conservatives are on the side of the lords and barons.... We at The Weekly Standard are pulling up the drawbridge against the peasants.

William Kristol, 1996

George W. Bush's great-grandfather, Samuel Prescott Bush, was a steel magnate, the first president of the National Manufacturers Association, a founding member of the United States Chamber of Commerce, and a top official of the War Industries Board during World War I. His grandfather, Prescott Sheldon Bush, was a graduate of Yale, an investment banker in New York, and a senator from Connecticut. His father, George Herbert Walker Bush, was a graduate of Yale, an oil executive, a congressman, the chairman of the Republican National Committee, the head of the Central Intelligence Agency, vice president of the United States, and finally president of the same. Bush himself, before becoming president, was a graduate of Yale, an oil executive, a business owner, and governor of Texas.

Through four generations, the Bush family has never left the lower right, where the dominant interests are always order, stability, prosperity, and power. In most societies, these interests supersede all other concerns. They are especially dear to the well-to-do, who have the most to gain or lose, but they are also the concern of many people of modest means who find that the established order works for them and who therefore wish to see it strengthened.

In the early American experience, the lower right has put forth a succession of political parties representing established interests: the Federalist Party of Alexander Hamilton, the National Republican Party of John Quincy Adams, the Whigs led by Henry Clay and Daniel Webster, and finally the Republican Party of Abraham Lincoln. Each of these parties backed a strong national government, a strong chief executive, and what Clay called the "American system" of central banking, protective tariffs, cheap immigrant labor, and federal funding of internal improvements like roads and canals to benefit commerce and industry.

The lower right had its heyday in the Gilded Age following the Civil War, but in the Progressive Era of the early 1900s, it was forced to accept a range of reforms affecting business (labor laws, financial regulation, antitrust restrictions, food and drug standards, prohibition), along with other measures meant to democratize the political system such as direct election of senators and female suffrage. The Great Depression brought another round of unwelcome reforms and regulations, which the lower right resisted until its fear of socialism passed and it started making money again. After World War II, the lower right continued to resist additional burdens but gave up the fight against the New Deal. Its conservatism was of the go-slow variety, not fixed on ancient truths but content with the status quo and cautious about change. It was pro-business but not otherwise ideological, often treating political differences as matters of mere prudence.

To a young Cold Warrior named William F. Buckley Jr., the lower right in the 1950s seemed all too willing to follow the lower left into outright socialism. To keep this from happening, Buckley founded *National Review*, which aimed to convert the East Coast elite to the cause of anti-communism. In its first issue, Buckley declared that the magazine "stands athwart history, yelling Stop." The *National Review* was for the Cold War and against the New Deal, taking a largely laissez-faire, anti-collectivist stance on economics. In its early years, it was also a platform for Frank Meyer's "fusionism," with its equal emphasis on political liberty and personal virtue. Meyer believed this "joint heritage" distinguished American conservatism from the authoritarian conservatism of Europe. "In a sense," he wrote, "we American conservatives are at the same time both Tory and Whig, both traditionalist and libertarian."[1]

But Buckley himself was always much more of a Tory. He had some early Old Right influences. His father had been friends with Albert Jay Nock, founder of *The Freeman* in the 1920s and author of *Our Enemy, the State.* But Buckley's personal style and vision was old-world and upper-class, notwithstanding his oft-noted libertarian streak. As an Anglophile, Buckley was an admirer of royalty and empire. As an Ivy Leaguer, he was too close to the East Coast elite not to want to be closer. As a Roman Catholic, he grieved for the Catholic kingdoms that fell victim to communism and backed vigorous use of American power to free them. As a student of Yale's Willmoore Kendall, he saw danger in the "open society" of John Stuart Mill and Karl Popper, which would have given a pass to card-carrying Communists working to overthrow the American order.[2]

Buckley could not have fought the fight against "un-American activities" without sharing Kendall's criticisms of classical liberalism and its modern egalitarian variants. Kendall was a twentieth-century Federalist who believed in limits to democracy, equality, and civil rights. He taught that no text better expressed the American political tradition than *The Federalist Papers* by Alexander Hamilton, James Madison, and John Jay. Kendall faulted Abraham Lincoln for wrongly giving first place to the Declaration of Independence and making too much of its mention of equality. He believed in the "deliberative process" by which leading persons could arrive at a just consensus representing Hamilton's "cool and deliberate sense of the community" (*Federalist* No. 63) within an established "public orthodoxy" (Kendall's words).[3]

For all his labors, Buckley never fully succeeded in winning over the lower right to his personal orthodoxy. The Republican establishment continued to resist his more ideological conservatism right up until 1980, when it was forced to accept Ronald Reagan as the GOP standard-bearer. When the lower right finally did embrace a conservative ideology in the 1980s, it did not embrace Buckley's Anglo-Catholic conservatism, but a new ideology called *neoconservatism.*

Books have been written about the neoconservatives, but they all concern a small subset of the larger category to be covered in this chapter. The set and subset have a lot in common, so it was only a matter of time before the one found the other. (To keep them separate, I will use uppercase when writing of the set and lowercase when writing of the subset.)

The original neoconservatives were big-city liberals who had been "mugged by reality," as Irving Kristol famously put it. Some had been

Marxists or Trotskyists before their muggings, others merely liberals or centrists. Many were Jews who were inspired by the founding of Israel in 1948 to become Cold War hawks. All were generally content with post-war America, but increasingly skeptical of government efforts to solve social problems. They were also alarmed by the Left's unwillingness to admit the evils of Stalinism and by the rise of the countercultural New Left in the 1960s, which they feared would undermine the bourgeois values that held society together.

The early neocons could not convert to then current forms of American conservatism because those forms were largely based on people, places, and things they did not know and love. A century ago, the lower right was self-consciously white, Anglo-Saxon, and Protestant. It was not especially religious and suspected Catholics of disloyalty and fundamentalists of fanaticism. It was proud of its culture and looked down on outsiders. It welcomed immigrants as cheap labor, but worried about the ill effects of alien races and insisted on "Americanization." Some in the lower right were inclined toward social Darwinism; others embraced racial theories and eugenics (also popular in the lower left at the time).

By mid-century, however, the lower right's WASP self-consciousness was on the wane. This was partly a result of leftist attacks on its racial, cultural, and class pretensions, so out of fashion after World War II, but it was also an inevitable consequence of the growing ethnic diversity of the business world, which every year was less and less WASP.

The loss of its WASP self-consciousness accentuated an age-old problem for the lower right: how to rationalize its political dominance. In every age, the lower right is a league of interests in need of an ideology. Federalism, Union, and Manifest Destiny served it well in the country's first hundred years, but nothing empowered the lower right to keep progressivism at bay in the twentieth century. The social upheavals of the 1960s were especially challenging. The lower right had no coherent defense against the revolutionary demands of the New Left and was increasingly inclined to follow the Left on most issues, just as Buckley feared.

The early neoconservatives offered not a ready-made ideology, but a set of preferred principles and an approach to problems consistent with the lower right's basic values and interests. The neocon approach concentrated on the practical problem of actually winning politically and making policy. It was flexible and pragmatic, not doctrinaire or idealistic. It sought acceptance and common ground, rather than confrontation and complete victory, even while re-framing the debate to its own advantage. It was realistic about what it could accomplish, and it based its arguments as much as possible on empirical evidence from the social sciences, not on tradition, religion, or philosophy.

The neocons' principles were never set forth in single manifesto, but they are not hard to discern. In his 1996 book *The Neoconservative Vision*, Mark Gerson, later a speechwriter for President George W. Bush, identified four fundamental Neocon beliefs: (1) life is too complex and our understanding of it too limited to place much faith in designs for a perfect world; (2) human nature is a mix of good and bad, self-interest and altruism, which makes progress possible but perfection impossible; (3) man is necessarily a social animal whose freedom "must serve the larger end of societal virtue"; and (4) "Ideas rule the world," and societies must defend their defining principles or "fall prey to the forces intent on subverting or altering those principles."[4]

To Gerson's list, we could add at least two more: (5) people vary greatly in abilities, opportunities, and ambitions, which makes "equality of outcomes" an inappropriate object of public policy and (6) a free market is the best source of material wealth but not a model for all social life. In sum, the early neocons were anti-utopian, anti-egalitarian, anti-communist, and anti-individualist; also pro-state, pro-business, pro-community, and pro-American.

Still, their movement into the lower right was slow. One problem was the conservative label, with which they were not entirely comfortable. " 'Neo-liberal' would perhaps have been a more accurate label for the entire group than neo-conservative," Norman Podhoretz wrote in 1979, "except for the fact that its liberalism was old and not new—that is, it derived from the New Deal and not from the New Politics."[5]

Another problem was their concern for the effects of capitalism on society. The lower right had learned to live with the regulation of business; it had also accepted responsibility for the welfare state, a modern *noblesse oblige* that only impossible ideologues still opposed; but it had not made the connection between capitalism and cultural decline. The ex-Marxist Neocons had. Marx taught that capitalism would ultimately undermine the bourgeois values that sustain it. Family, religion, community, art—everything would fall victim to the market's unsparing efficiency, to be either bought and sold or discarded as worthless. For this reason, the Neocons could offer only "two cheers for capitalism," by Irving Kristol's count. Kristol writes:

Adam Smith himself, though a creative genius in economic thought, was something of a philistine, believing that cultural attitudes and opinions, like religious ones, were matters of personal taste about which reasonable men would not and should not get particularly excited. For two centuries now, Western civilization has been haunted by this stupendous error of judgment, with the result that today, even as a market economy is accepted as superior to any other, at least in principle, the bourgeois society on which the market economy is based is being challenged with unprecedented boldness and success.[6]

The neocons' Moses—the man with the message who made their movement into the lower right not only possible but necessary—was Leo Strauss. A German Jew from an Orthodox family, Strauss worked at the Academy of Jewish Research in Berlin until 1932, when the Nazis came to power. Emigrating to the United States in 1938, he taught first at the New School for Social Research in New York, then at the University of Chicago. After retiring from there in 1968, he was honored with teaching positions at Claremont Men's College in California and St. John's College in Maryland.

Few men have been as influential in their corners as Leo Strauss was in the lower right. Willmoore Kendall declared Strauss "*the* great teacher of political philosophy, not of our time alone, but of any time since Machiavelli"; his works were "not required reading but scripture for everyone who likes to think of himself as a conservative."[7] Irving Kristol has more than once confessed his debt to Strauss in the highest possible terms:

Encountering Strauss's work produced the kind of intellectual shock that is a once-in-a-lifetime experience. He turned one's intellectual universe upside down. Suddenly, one realized that one had been looking at the history of Western political thought through the wrong end of the telescope.[8]

Strauss died in 1973, but his teaching is more alive than ever. He established not only his own school of political theory, but his own cult-like following. Kristol writes, "His students—those happy few who sat at his feet—became 'Straussians,' though they preferred to be known as 'political theorists.' (One such student was my dear friend, the late Martin Diamond, who helped me understand what Strauss was up to.)"[9]

If Strauss is not more widely known, it is because his teaching was never intended for a popular audience, but for a happy few who are morally and intellectually deserving. Exclusivity is the key to Strauss's thought. There are, he taught, two ways to live: the philosopher's way and the people's way. The philosopher's way is better, but few can follow it because few can bear the truth of philosophy. Kristol writes that Strauss did not believe "the Enlightenment dogma that 'the truth will make men free.'" Instead, he believed that the truth will make most men hopeless and therefore dangerous. Kristol again:

He was an intellectual aristocrat who thought that the truth could make *some* minds free, but he was convinced that there was an inherent conflict between philosophic truth and the political order, and that popularization and vulgarization of these truths might import unease, turmoil, and the release of popular passions hitherto held in check by tradition and religion—with utterly unpredictable, but mostly negative, consequences.[10]

Strauss taught that the great philosophers of the ancient world up through the Middle Ages believed this and taught it in such a way that only the deserving would understand. "One therefore had to study—not read—their texts with a quasi-'talmudic' intensity and care, in order to distinguish between their 'esoteric' and 'exoteric' views," writes Kristol. Strauss himself wrote this way, so that only the initiated would know, as Kristol says, what he was up to. This was the "Great Tradition" of Western political philosophy, whose public aim was not to spread the truth, but to humble the people before the intellectual aristocracy. Strauss wrote, "The basic premise of classical political philosophy may be said to be the view that natural inequality of the intellectual powers is, or ought to be, of decisive political importance."[11]

The Great Tradition began to break down with Machiavelli, who throws off the veil of religion and morality and plainly tells his prince how to rule ruthlessly. Later writers like Thomas Hobbes and Baruch Spinoza do more damage by plainly telling the people how to ruthlessly overthrow their princes. In time, modern rationalistic political philosophy, shorn of all piety and faith, degenerates into positivism, then historicism, and ultimately nihilism and Nietzsche's "will to power," responsible for the murderous utopian tyrannies of the twentieth century. Strauss believed that this "crisis of the West" was brought on by the popular application of reason to matters of truth and justice. "The more we cultivate reason," he wrote, "the more we cultivate nihilism: the less we are able to be loyal members of society. The inescapable practical consequence of nihilism is fanatical obscurantism."[12]

Strauss's critique of modernity held special significance to many neocons because modernity denied not only the Christian Gospel, but also all meaning to Jewishness. Through the lens of reason, thoroughgoing moderns could only see Jewishness and especially Zionism as another racist, irrational, and repressive nationalism. Strauss therefore believed Jews could safely remain Jews only if people respected nonrational traditions, religions, and cultures, as the pre-modern West had.

Straussians disagree on how America fits into the scheme of history. The so-called East Coast Straussians see America as a "proposition nation," based not on historical ethnic or religious values, but on the specific principles declared by the Founders and propounded by heroic leaders like

Lincoln. The so-called West Coast Straussians see America as a revival and culmination of the classical and biblical tradition of Natural Law, which reconciles Reason and Revelation, Athens and Jerusalem. Either way, the challenge is to tame the nation by correcting its tendencies toward tyrannous utopianism, chaotic individualism, and divisive traditionalism—the dangers of the lower left, the upper left, and the upper right, respectively.

To that end, these new Neoconservatives have made political allies of the Religious Right, backing Richard John Neuhaus after his break with the Rockford Institute, publicly defending Pat Robertson and the Christian Coalition, and once lauding Gary Bauer as a conservative champion. Policy-wise, Neocons have joined Theocons in backing bans on cloning and fetal-tissue research, tighter controls on vice and indecency, public support of faith-based social programs, more choice in education, and more room for religion in public life. They have even joined Theocons in attacking the anti-religious assumptions of Darwinian evolution as taught in public schools.

On the other hand, Neocons have sorely disappointed Theocons on touchy social issues like abortion and gay rights. There are two reasons for this: one is that the practical, power-minded Neocons pick and choose their battles, preferring those with better odds; the other is that Neocons are not as motivated by religious obligation as Theocons are. This is on account of the Neocons' Straussian regard for morality and religion, which is highly instrumental. Religion is good for people because it keeps them from despair and gives them rules to live by; it does not, however, hand down prescriptive dictates that societies or individuals are obliged to defend at all cost.[13] It matters less to Neocons that a religion's metaphysical claims are true than that its claims support the good order and discipline of the people. Religion's worth is in its "noble lie" that intellectual aristocrats like Strauss are not obliged to believe but are obliged to respect by keeping their doubts or disbelief to themselves. Irving Kristol explains:

There are in Washington today dozens of people who are married with children and religiously observant. Do they have faith? Who knows? They just believe that it is good to go to church or synagogue. Whether you believe or not is not the issue—that's between you and God—whether you are a member of a community that holds certain truths sacred, that is the issue.[14]

The primacy of membership in a group takes us back to the Latin roots of the word *religion*: from *religio* (respect for what is sacred), from *religare* (to tie, to fasten behind), from *re-* (back or again) and *ligare* (to bind or to bind together). In fact, the lower right's regard for religion is very Roman, stressing values that make people good and honorable citizens and soldiers.

In his best-seller *The Book of Virtues*, Neocon moralist William Bennett names ten virtues in this order: self-discipline, compassion, responsibility, friendship, work, courage, perseverance, honesty, loyalty, and faith. Of the last, Bennett writes:

. . . religious faith adds a significant dimension to the moral life of humanity world-wide. Faith is a source of discipline and power and meaning in the lives of the faithful of any major religious creed. It is a potent force in human experience. A shared faith binds people together in ways that cannot be duplicated by other means.[15]

Bennett leaves out one important Roman virtue—modesty. He also skips an essential Christian virtue—humility. Both are out of fashion to-day, but their omission is better explained by the broadly ecumenical scope of Bennett's book, subtitled *A Treasury of Great Moral Stories*. Neocons are never evangelists for any particular religion, though they do often ap-peal to a vague "Judeo-Christian tradition," the lower right's preferred faith since the mid-twentieth century. "The fate of our democracy is inti-mately intertwined—'entangled,' if you will—with the vitality of the Judeo-Christian tradition," Bennett writes. Some have lately tried to update this faith to the "Abramic tradition" so as to draw Muslims to the right side of the War on Terror. The point is still that the state cannot be strictly neutral in matters of faith, for, Bennett writes, "Neutrality to religion turns out to bring with it neutrality to those values that issue from religion."[16] The Neocon regard for religion is not neutrality but plurality, as in the words of an earlier inhabitant of the lower right (Dwight Eisenhower), often quoted for their irreligious irony: "Our form of government has no sense unless it is founded in a deeply felt religious faith, and I don't care what it is."

Despite this emphasis on religion, the major elements of the Neocons' public orthodoxy are strictly secular and all intended to tighten the national bond among peoples of different races, religions, ethnicities, etc. Their holy scriptures are the "Great Books" of the "Western canon," from which we distill our modern American values. Neocons see America as a "proposi-tional nation," defined not by its land and people, but by its dedication to the high ideals of its founding documents and national heroes, which Neocons regard with rarely critical reverence. Their scholarship aims not to get at the unflattering facts of American history, but to preserve a useful national heritage against assaults upon it from the Left. Their first concern is *Making Patriots*, the title of a recent book by Walter Berns of the American Enterprise Institute.

In this, Neocons differ sharply from Paleocons, who judge the American experience by more idealistic, less pragmatic standards and are therefore more critical of it. Paleocons, for instance, are inclined to believe that Thomas Jefferson fathered children by his slave girl Sally Hemings; Neocons have denounced this claim as an ideologically motivated slander against a founding father. Many Paleocons revile the names of Abraham Lincoln, Franklin Roosevelt, and Martin Luther King Jr.; Neocons honor them dutifully and denounce the Paleocons for their impiety.

Nowadays Neocons don't have to do much denouncing of Paleocons. They won the war against the Old Right. They drove diehards like Joseph Sobran, Lew Rockwell, Thomas Fleming, and finally Patrick Buchanan from the political battlefield and forced all Paleocons and Paleolibs who wished to remain to accept the limitations of the new conservative orthodoxy, which by the mid-1990s was so secure that the Neocons themselves announced the "end of neoconservatism." What had been neoconservatism had become mere conservatism, of the kind advanced by such mainstream conservative sources as Rush Limbaugh, Bill O'Reilly, Fox News, *The Washington Times*, *National Review*, the Heritage Foundation, the American Enterprise Institute, the Hoover Institution, the Hudson Institute, the Ethics and Public Policy Center, the Center for Security Policy, and the Republican National Committee. As Norman Podhoretz declared in his 1996 "eulogy" to neoconservatism, "what killed neoconservatism was not defeat but victory."[17]

The victory of the Neos was all the easier because the Paleos were never fully in control of the conservative movement and never very influential in the lower right, for the simple reason that Paleo ideals do not serve lower-right interests. Those interests have not changed much over time, though some circumstances have, and the lower right has changed with them. Free trade has replaced protectionism as the national business strategy, Jews have replaced WASP's as the dominant ethnic group, and Israel has replaced England as our dearest cousin across the Pond.

What the new Neocons have accomplished is the rationalization of the lower right's political dominance. They have restored the lower right's confidence in its claim to power, founded this claim on values and interests congenial to most twenty-first-century Americans, and put forth a political strategy for actually winning elections and making policy.

The old conservative orthodoxy had rested on three pillars: traditional values, limited government, and anti-communism, or, in the words of Rich Lowry, Buckley's handpicked successor as editor of *National Review*, "libertarian economics with traditionalism on moral issues and staunch anti-communism." The new orthodoxy replaced these with three pillars of greater importance to the lower right: Irving Kristol's "religion, nationalism and economic growth." The substitutions are telling: a specific tradition gives way to an unspecific religion, aggressive nationalism takes the place of anti-communism, and economic growth trumps limited government and libertarian economics. Dinesh D'Souza has ventured an even vaguer conservative trinity: "prosperity, security, and social decency." Others on the right might like something more definitive. (Who, after all, is for poverty, danger, and indecency?) But it is on D'Souza's level that the Republican Party successfully appeals to American voters.[18]

Together these three new pillars hold up the edifice of "democratic capitalism," the name given to the export version of the Neocon worldview. Michael Novak, chief apostle of democratic capitalism, defines it as "three systems in one: a predominantly market economy; a polity respectful of the rights of the individual to life, liberty, and the pursuit of happiness; and a system of cultural institutions moved by ideals of liberty and justice for all." Says Novak, "Democratic capitalism is not just a system but a way of life. Its ethos includes a special evolution of pluralism; respect for contingency and unintended consequences; a sense of sin; and a new and distinctive conception of community, the individual, and the family."[19]

To Novak, the ideal of democratic capitalism is not the welfare state but the "welfare society," which avoids both "the excessive individualism of *laissez-faire* and the excessive collectivism of social democracy." To Kristol, this means a limited "paternal welfare state," as opposed to an unlimited "maternal welfare state," which is "inherently expansive—compassion has no limits—and sooner or later it runs into economic counterpressures." To George W. Bush, this means the difference between a "culture of dependency" and "the responsibility era" in which people take responsibility for themselves and others:

I want to usher in the responsibility era, an era when every American knows with certainty that each of us is responsible for our actions, that each of us is responsible for our family and our community, that each of us is responsible for loving a neighbor as we would like to be loved ourselves.[20]

The responsibility era does not mean laissez faire, for, Bush writes, "Government can be a part of helping usher in the responsibility era. Government sends signals every day." In practical terms, this means national service programs, federal funding for local education, more choice in education but also national education standards, and support for faith-based social programs, all out of concern for the bourgeois values that undergird our democratic-capitalist way of life.[21]

Neocons are for both Big Government and Big Business. They trust and encourage business interests, but they also accept that a fair degree of regulation is required by today's complex global economy. They wouldn't dare disrupt the markets by abolishing the Federal Reserve System or returning to the gold standard. They support free trade and global markets, along with the international arrangements that facilitate them. They resist assaults on commerce by envious populists, defensive nationalists, and destructive anarchists. They generally side with industry on environmental matters. They often look to cut taxes and boost spending at the same time, trusting the growing economy to pay for the growing government. The concern is to get the government doing the right things, to have less government in some areas but more government in other areas, especially national security. Kristol admits that paternal welfare states tend to spend more on defense, but he argues that the United States has no other choice: it cannot "opt out of world affairs." Besides, he says, Americans are quite keen on their military.[22] Some Neocons are even keener.

But an aggressive foreign policy is only part of the lower right's aspiration to "national greatness," praised by David Brooks of *The Weekly Standard* and damned by Marvin Olasky of *World* magazine. Brooks favors "limited but energetic" government leading the country on a "national mission" in which all Americans will find meaning and purpose. "Historically," he writes, "national missions have including settling the West, building the highway system, creating the post-war science faculties, exploring space, waging the Cold War, and disseminating American culture throughout the world." But however worthy these tasks might be, what matters most is the healing effect of common purpose on the American people. In words that recall the romantic nationalisms of the nineteenth century, Brooks writes:

It almost doesn't matter what great task government sets for itself, as long as it does some tangible thing with energy and effectiveness. The first task of government is to convey a spirit of confidence and vigor that can then spill across the life of the nation. Stagnant government drains national morale. A government that fails to offer any vision merely feeds public cynicism and disenchantment.

But energetic government is good for its own sake. It raises the sights of the individual. It strengthens common bonds. It boosts national pride. It continues the great national project. It allows each generation to join the work of their parents. The quest for national greatness defines the word "American" and makes it new for every generation.[23]

At this point, the lower right's concern for religion and morality gives way to the desire for national unity, purpose, prosperity, and power. Conservatism becomes inclusive and reformist and increasingly focused on corporatist endeavors like national service, global peacekeeping, the War on Terror, world trade, and the triumph of the American will worldwide.

Outside the circle, deep in the lower right, we find the Next Generation Neocons at the Project for a New American Century and *The Weekly Standard*. These are bold Young Turks who are not afraid to urge on us an American empire. The empire they have in mind is not like the British or Roman Empires, with colonies and provinces ruled directly from the capital. Instead, their model is the Athenian Empire in the fifth century before Christ, a league of prosperous, democratic allies dominated by its most prosperous and democratic member, just as Athens dominated the Delian League before the city's defeat in the Peloponnesian Wars (which democratic Athens started).

Until the terrorist attacks of September 11, 2001, they weren't quite up to calling it an empire. The closest any of them came was an "American imperium" (Irving Kristol). As early as 1996, William Kristol and Robert Kagan were recommending "benevolent global hegemony" for the propagation of American values throughout the world. They called this stance "neo-Reaganite," but they had little use for Reagan's "charming old metaphor of the United States as a 'city on a hill.'. . . a policy of sitting atop a hill and leading by example in practice is a policy of cowardice and dishonor."[24]

Then, amid the alarm of 9-11, the Young Turks grew bolder and began to advocate empire openly. Barely a month after the attacks, Max Boot was urging America "to embrace its imperial role" as the "most realistic response." Against those who argued that the attacks were payback for American imperialism, Boot argued in *The Weekly Standard*, "The September 11 attack was a result of insufficient American involvement and ambition; the solution is to be more expansive in our goals and more assertive in their implementation." The foreign-born Boot wrote admiringly of the British empire in the nineteenth century, when the collapse of various Middle Eastern regimes obliged the British to "quell the resulting disorder." Today the same lands "cry out for the sort of enlightened foreign administration once provided by self-confident Englishmen in jodhpurs and pith helmets." Boot had already set his sights on two countries to be conquered, Afghanistan because of the Taliban's support for Osama bin Laden and Iraq because Saddam Hussein was "working to acquire weapons of mass destruction that he or his confederates will unleash against America and our allies [Israel] if given the chance." He imagined that invading Americans would "probably have plenty of help from Iraqis" and that afterward the United States would "enjoy fruitful cooperation from the region's many opportunists."[25]

Such talk served its purpose—it got us into Afghanistan and Iraq. Since then even the boldest Neocons have toned down their talk of empire, amid the continuing unrest in Iraq and the failure to find weapons of mass destruction. Neocons themselves have come under greater public scrutiny and taken considerable heat for urging war. Much of the heat has focused on the attachment of leading Neoconservatives to Israel. Naturally, Patrick Buchanan was among the hottest, writing at the peak of pre-war passions:

> *Cui Bono*? For whose benefit these endless wars in a region that holds nothing vital to America save oil, which the Arabs must sell us to survive? Who would benefit from a war of civilizations between the West and Islam? Answer: one nation, one leader, one party. Israel, Sharon, Likud.[26]

As Bush's former speechwriter David Frum would point out, the words "one nation, one leader, one party" echoed the Nazi slogan *Ein Volk, ein Reich, ein Führer*. The implication was impossible to miss: Buchanan was likening Neocon Zionists to German fascists.

It was an indication of how hot it had become for Neoconservatives that Frum felt the need to respond publicly by condemning Paleocons in the pages of *National Review*, even naming names of the very nonpersons Neocons had been trying to get conservatives to forget—Pat Buchanan, Robert Novak, Llewellyn Rockwell, Samuel Francis, Thomas Fleming, Scott McConnell, Justin Raimondo, Joe Sobran, Charley Reese, Jude Wanniski, Eric Margolis, and Taki Theodoracopulos. Frum accused them all of treason:

> They have made common cause with the left-wing and Islamist antiwar movements in this country and in Europe. They deny and excuse terror. They espouse a potentially self-fulfilling defeatism. They publicize wild conspiracy theories. And some of them explicitly yearn for the victory of their nation's enemies.[27]

In a lengthy article (over 6,400 words), Frum rehearsed the whole story of the paleocon/neocon rift in the Reagan administration, then zeroed in on the Paleocons' criticism of Israel and Neoconservative support for Israel. He then delivered a final anathema: "War is a great clarifier. It forces people to take sides. The paleoconservatives have chosen—and the rest of us must choose too. In a time of danger, they have turned their backs on their country. Now we turn our backs on them."

But Paleoconservatives were not alone in their criticism of the Neoconservative enthusiasm for war. Many people otherwise at home in the Neocon corner opposed the war and doubted the motives of Neocon hawks. These included well-known foreign policy "realists" like Brent Scowcroft, a retired Air Force general and national security advisor to President George H.W. Bush, and Andrew Bacevich, a retired Army colonel and professor of international relations at Boston University. Scowcroft declared his misgivings in *The New Yorker* magazine, while Bacevich became a contributing editor of *The American Conservative*, founded by Pat Buchanan and Taki Theodoracopulos but edited by another former Neocon, Scott McConnell. Concern about Israeli influence in American foreign policy also motivated a daring exposé of the "Israel lobby" by John J. Mearsheimer of the University of Chicago and Stephen Walt of Harvard. The organizations and individuals mentioned as active participants in the lobby read like a who's who of the Neocon foreign policy establishment.[28]

Yet the only notable Neocon known to have confessed a change of heart on account of the Iraq War is Francis Fukuyama of the School of Advanced International Studies at Johns Hopkins University. Fukuyama carried nearly impeccable Neocon credentials. He was a student of Allan Bloom, a protégé of Leo Strauss; he worked with Robert Wohlstetter, another influential protégé of Strauss; and he had worked with Paul Wolfowitz, a protégé of Richard Perl and neocon point man within the Defense Department. Fukuyama rose to national fame with a post-Cold War article touting the "end of history," which became the 1992 book *The End of History and the Last Man*. The article and book heralded a new era of modern, liberal, democratic capitalism.

Until the Iraq War, Fukuyama fit well among the neocons, identifying with what he saw as neoconservatism's realistic means of achieving idealistic ends. But in the years after the 2003 invasion of Iraq, Fukuyama began to think that something had gone wrong. The younger generation were not so realistic about their means. Fukuyama attributed this in part to "overoptimism" following the success of a hardline American foreign policy in facing down the Soviet Union. The younger Neocons prided themselves in their "hard Wilsonianism," in the words of Max Boot, which they contrasted with the "soft Wilsonianism" of the progressive Left. The difference is that the latter looks to international law, foreign aid, and multilateral efforts to democratize the world, while the former relies more heavily on the unilateral exercise of American military might. Since American hegemony was so obviously benevolent, these "hard Wilsonians" expected that the world would be amazed by American power without feeling threatened by it.

Fukuyama called this expectation "absurd." He declared his break with Neoconservatism in March 2006, writing in the *New York Times* that "Neoconservatism, as both a political symbol and a body of thought, has evolved into something I can no longer support." Fukuyama did not deal directly with the issue of Israel, but he did mention the Trotskyite past of many early

Jewish Neocons and even faulted younger Neocons like William Kristol and Robert Kagan for their "Leninism," that is to say, their belief that "history can be pushed along with the right application of power and will." Yet even while disowning their methods, he approved of their objectives:

The problem with neoconservatism's agenda lies not in its ends, which are as American as apple pie, but rather in the overmilitarized means by which it has sought to accomplish them. What American foreign policy needs is not a return to a narrow and cynical realism, but rather the formulation of a "realistic Wilsonianism" that better matches means to ends.[29]

Believing that the Neocon moment has passed, Fukuyama worries that its foreign-policy excesses will lead Americans away from the Wilsonian commitment to spreading democracy, toward isolationism.

It should be remembered that while attachment to Israel and aggressive foreign policy are characteristic of today's Neoconservatism, they are not essential to it. It is therefore possible to be a Neoconservative and neither a hawk nor a Zionist, although those in the farthest reaches of the lower right are almost always both.

Chapter 11

Postmodern Populism

We recommend that you should try to get what it is possible for you to get, taking into consideration what we both really do think; since you know as well as we do that, when these matters are discussed by practical people, the standard of justice depends on the equality of power to compel and that in fact the strong do what they have the power to do and the weak accept what they have to accept.

The Athenians to the Melians, 416 B.C.

The world has changed much since the terrorist attacks of September 11, 2001, and one of the more recent changes is that James Webb is again a Democrat. The best-selling novelist and Marine combat veteran was assistant secretary of Defense and then secretary of the Navy in the Republican administration of Ronald Reagan. He was gung-ho for the Reagan military build-up and even resigned as Navy secretary because he could not publicly support the administration's retreat from its goal of a 600-ship Navy. Webb was also a hero among military officers for his public opposition to women in combat, bluntly stated in a magazine article titled "Women Can't Fight." But Webb publicly opposed both the Gulf War and the Iraq War. The latter was enough to move this former "Reagan Democrat" to run for the United States Senate as a Virginia Democrat.

The move surprised many of Webb's conservative fans. They could understand his outspokenness against the war. The Marine Corps, in fact, has a long tradition of iconoclastic straight-talkers determined to shake the system: Major General Smedley Butler railed against the commercial interests he saw behind U.S. interventions in Central America; Colonel

Evans Carlson sided with the Communist Chinese against the Nationalist Chinese in World War II (even popularizing in America the Communist slogan *gung-ho*, meaning "work together"); former Commandant General David Shoup spoke and wrote against the Vietnam War; and, most recently, General Anthony Zinni has drawn impolitic attention to the importance of Israel to key proponents of the Iraq War.

Webb's take on the Iraq War is similar. "This doctrine of preemptive war is not American," he declares, adding that "those people who are doing this have more in common with the Soviet Union than they do with the United States."[1] He does not say just who "those people" are, but the implication is obvious to those in the know: He means the ex-Trotskyite neoconservatives, many of whom are Jews and all of whom are Zionists.

But Webb is no Buchananite. Instead, he is a quintessential populist, idealistic to a fault but indifferent to religion, middle class in his perspective but independent in his thinking, and moderate in his views about almost everything. "I'm like a lot of people who left the Democratic Party at the end of the Vietnam War, principally on national security issues," he says. "I never really found a home in the Republican party because of, in my view, extreme positions on social issues."[2]

Webb identifies his two guiding themes as fairness and privacy, meaning by the latter that "the government's power stops at the individual's front door."[3] He is therefore pro-choice on abortion and pro-gun on the Second Amendment. He approves of gay rights except in the military and civil unions for gays but not marriage. He is for fair trade, public schooling, universal health care, and more equitable taxation.[4] He sees in today's politics too much ideology and too little leadership: "There are times, I think, where it's more important to have really creative, affirmative leadership, and I think this is one of those times."[5]

Webb believes the future lies with the traditional Democratic Party base and hopes his candidacy will bring "working-class white folk" back into the party. He sees himself as a political outsider. When he left the Pentagon in 1987, he asked to have his name removed from Washington's social register. "I have no desire in my life to go to those parties," he says. "I am not of Washington at all. I understand it, I know it, but I am not of it." His most recent book is a history of his Celtic forebears, entitled *Born Fighting*. "It's about the Scots-Irish," he says, "but it's really about the evolution of populist democracy; it came right out of this culture."[6] "Born Fighting" is also his campaign slogan.

Unfortunately for Webb, quite a few of his Celtic kin responded with atavistic bellicosity to the terrorist attacks of 9-11 and strongly supported the prosecution of the "war on terror" through Afghanistan and Iraq. How long they will continue to do so remains to be seen. Polls show a steady decline in support for the war, but people take a long time to admit they were wrong, and the white folks Webb counts as kin have other reasons not to rejoin the Democratic Party.

By now, it should be obvious how the eight perspectives shake out on Election Day. Democrats dominate the lower left, taking in virtually all Progressives and pulling heavily among Communitarians and Radicals. In contrast, Republicans cast a wider ideological net, pulling heavily in the three other corners of our Compass. If voters were evenly distributed across the Compass, the GOP might easily claim two thirds of the electorate. But most votes, following most money, are found below the A axis, and so the match is much more even.

Still, the GOP has managed to turn its ideological diversity into an electoral advantage by basing the party's appeal on the two main concerns of the nation as a whole: economic prosperity and national security. To these concerns, Republicans have subordinated their secondary concerns for family values and limited government. They have also adopted a strategy of appeasement on social spending for things like education and health care, which has at least halved the appeal of Democrats' demands for more. These adjustments have allowed the GOP to spread its Big Tent farther across the Compass to take in more of the electorate's nonideological center. Satisfying everyone in the tent is always a challenge, but the assemblage of interests gives Republicans a rhetorical edge in public debate. They simply have more to say to draw voters.

By contrast, the Democratic Party's values and interests are too concentrated in the lower left to appeal to the entire electorate. The causes party activists care about most—abortion, affirmative action, gay rights, entitlement programs, environmentalism, and multiculturalism—do not top the list of concerns for most Americans in the twenty-first century. They are old "social justice" issues on which the Left has already largely had its way. Democrats can only now call for holding the line or doing even more—more spending on social services, more transfer payments to the poor, more advantages for preferred groups, more laws to protect the environment, and more public insistence on diversity. But none of these is an obvious winner with the American people, and some run directly contrary to public opinion.

The lower left has been able to hang on to power for so long because of its near monopoly in media, academia, the grant-giving foundations, and the government bureaucracy, including state and federal courts. "Put simply, there is more brain power on the Left, more money and more resources," write *The Economist*'s John Micklethwait and Adrian Wooldridge in *The*

Right Nation.[7] But in recent years, the courts have been curbed by a more conservative federal judiciary, and the lower left's media monopoly has been broken, first by talk radio, then by Fox News and the Internet. The uncertain economy and the terrorist attacks of September 11 have also worked to the Right's advantage, turning voters to the party that puts prosperity and security above all else.

The GOP is not assured of every success, of course. Bill Clinton has shown us what a savvy Svengali can accomplish when Democrats ease up on their own obsessions and Republicans overreach and make mistakes. President Bush has overreached already in Iraq, handing Democrats a club to beat him with. Republican bungling, corruption, and hubris can still spell disaster for the party.

Yet it would still seem that we have witnessed a historic shift of power from the lower left to the lower right, comparable to the Depression Era shift from the lower right to the lower left. Such a shift would likely last for decades. The lower right is, after all, power's natural position. Only in the modern age, the Age of Anarchy following the collapse of the Christian consensus on church and state, has power wandered anywhere else. Our basic scheme, with its four main political traditions, helps us to see how (see Figure 11.1).

POST-CHRISTIAN POWER SHIFTS

Many historians have tried to fit the political history of the United States into the narrative of a single authentically American tradition. Conservatives have stressed the country's heritage of ordered liberty and constitutionally limited self-government, surviving against the assault of progressive notions imported from abroad. Liberals sharing the so-called "liberal consensus" have assumed the Whig view of history and seen only progress toward greater and greater freedom and democracy. Marxists, following Richard Hofstadter, have dismissed said progress as largely illusory and stressed the permanency of a single socio-economic system in which rival interests merely compete for marginal advantage. Louis Hartz saw "irrational Lockeianism" as the root of a paradoxical Americanism mixing populist individualism and nationalistic conformism, while Leo Strauss encouraged an approach to American history designed to support a messianic nationalism based on faith in America's founding as a "proposition nation" destined for "national greatness."

The theory advanced in this book suggests another view, one that incorporates the insights of the various single-tradition narratives but avoids

Figure 11.1
Four Political Americans

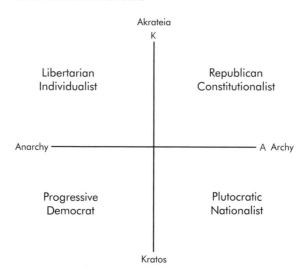

Akrateia

K

Libertarian
Individualist

Republican
Constitutionalist

Anarchy ——————————————— A Archy

Progressive
Democrat

Plutocratic
Nationalist

Kratos

their reductionist tendencies as well as their partisan bias. In this new view, the political history of the United States can be better explained on the basis of contention between the four divergent traditions identified in Chapter 1. Two constants of that contention are (a) the persistent strength of the lower right, representing the interests of organized wealth, and (b) the relative weakness of the upper right and upper left, which are never dominant and only influential within a coalition. These constants have ensured that the dominant power in the American politics is either one of the lower corners alone or a coalition of three corners against one of the lower corners.

We can see this happening through history, from the English Civil War through the American Revolution. Limiting ourselves to just the American experience, we can see that the triumph of Hamiltonian Federalism, following the adoption of the Constitution, provoked an anti-Federalist reaction, which was strengthened by the growing anti-Federalist populations on the frontier. Power shifted from the lower right to a coalition of vaguely defined republicans, democrats, and individualists, represented first by Thomas Jefferson's Democratic-Republicans and later by Andrew Jackson's Democrats.

The lower right did not regain firm control until 1860, when a split in the Democratic coalition opened the way for Abraham Lincoln's Republican Party, representing Northern commercial interests intent on preserving the "American system" of central banking, protective tariffs, cheap immigrant labor, and federal funding of public improvements to speed industrialization and commerce.

In the Civil War, the two sides embraced the traditions closest to their causes. The South fought for "Southern rights" and traditional society, uniting its conflicting characteristics of social hierarchy and personal independence (attributable in part to its mixed Anglo-Saxon and Celtic heritage). The North united the progressivism of the abolitionists to the unionism of the Republican Party. (Before the war, many abolitionists actually favored *Northern* secession to rid themselves of slavery.) Union victory gave the lower right complete control through Reconstruction.

Afterwards, the lower right faced a growing challenge from the other three quadrants, which were strengthened by swelling immigrant populations in the North, strong local economies in the West and Midwest, and persistent anti-Republican sentiment in the impoverished South. Out of this resistance came the Populist and Progressive movements, which succeeded in forcing the lower right to modify its program.

Power shifted decisively to the lower left—for the first time in American history—in the Great Depression, which incited broad popular support for government solutions to help workers and the poor. This shift pitted the lower left against an anti-New Deal coalition centered on the upper right, combining the concerns of business conservatives, conservative Progressives, and anti-government individualists.

After World War II, the lower-right business establishment made its peace with the New Deal and joined forces with the lower-left labor establishment to fight the Cold War and enjoy the post-war boom, at what Daniel Bell in 1960 called "the end of ideology."

But very soon the rise of the New Left, the Civil Rights movement, and the Sexual Revolution split the country between Left and Right. Government involvement in these battles and increasing taxation and regulation again pitted the lower left against the rest. Ronald Reagan won in 1980 by centering his coalition on the upper right, making "liberals" in government the enemy of freedom, prosperity, and family values. This again united three quadrants of our scheme against the lower left in a winning strategy that Republicans still use.

Today the GOP's focus on security and prosperity, plus limited government and family values, gives it control over the lower right, the upper right, and the upper left, leaving only the lower left to the Democratic Party. Confined to one corner, Democrats can have little hope of recapturing the country. Their range of appeal is too narrow.

And yet for the past many years—indeed, for the past many centuries— the general trend in the West has been away from the upper right and toward the lower left. These are the poles we often mean when we speak of Left and Right, which is why both freedom-minded individualists and money-minded plutocrats tend not to think of themselves as right-wing or left-wing. At other times, however, we say Left and Right and mean the left and right of our A axis, counting libertarians as leftists and corporations as conservative.

THE END OF ANARCHY?

Were things to continue as before, we might expect that in time the lower right's dominance would inspire such resistance in the other corners that together they might again mount a populist challenge to the reigning plutocracy. A host of worsening conditions could fuel such resistance: swelling debt, rising oil prices, the growing trade imbalance, the loss of jobs overseas, the unceasing importation of desperately cheap foreign labor, and the burdens of empire. Each of these threatens the prosperity and security that the lower right promises to remain in power.

But there are good reasons to believe that things will not continue as before, that we might instead be entering a new era in which the ideologies that inspired resistance to plutocratic power in the Age of Anarchy will lose their appeal and fade into history.

The first reason is that the three corners in opposition to the lower right are now so far apart from each other that alliances between them are all but impossible. Recent years have witnessed a falling out between Left and Right libertarians, the failure of the Paleocon/Paleo'tarian alliance, the pitiful fortunes and changing faces of the populist Reform Party, and the Green Party's failed rebellion against Progressive participation in globalization and imperialism. 9-11 did as much to sharpen these divisions as it did to heal them. Only a catastrophe of much greater magnitude might possibly overcome them. Minor emergencies have tended only to strengthen the grip of the regime already in power.

The second reason is the growing weakness of both the upper right and the lower left. The weakness of the upper right is obvious to all. The corner can claim vindication by recent events, which have pointed up the dangers of open borders and foreign attachments. It still shows signs of intellectual life, with the founding of a new moderately Paleocon political magazine, *The American Conservative*, to complement the high-brow cultural critique of the Rockford Institute's *Chronicles*. But the corner, though rich with the ideas of past ages, still has few followers and little money. It is religiously divided, with "Celtic" Calvinism rivaling Roman

Catholicism for dominance. It still lacks a common understanding of the fundamental problem.

It is also increasingly out of step with postmodern America. The things it holds dear—Christian virtue and tradition, European history and culture, constitutional political theory, and patriarchal social order—no longer define America to the nation or to the world. The passions that do— secularism, commercialism, materialism, hedonism, optimism, futurism, chauvinism, imperialism, Zionism—the upper right regards as anathema. It can offer useful critiques of others' errors, but its own correctives are inadmissable in American politics because of choices made long ago at the nation's founding, choices that tied our fate not to "the permanent things" but to the future fashions of the *novus ordo seclorum.*

The weakness of the lower left is also obvious, but the depth of that weakness is debatable. The lower left has many followers and much money. It still dominates academia and maintains near total control of the enter- tainment industry, though its grip on the news media and the courts has loosened. It can still claim dominance in many parts of the country, and it continues to win battles on issues like gay marriage in those parts. But in other parts and at the national level, the lower left is in retreat. Its national leaders now openly fret about the Democratic Party's deepening identity crisis. "We are trying to decide what our core values are," says Democratic Senator Barack Obama of Illinois. "We've got to reassess ourselves. We've got to be born again," says Democratic strategist James Carville. "We know that we have principles," says Eli Pariser, executive director of MoveOn.org. "We need to get much more explicit about what those principles are. We need a coherent vision."

The lower left does indeed have principles, but economic growth and national security do not rank highly among them. The lower left also has core values—tolerance, diversity, equality, human rights—but these appear to more and more Americans as moralistic covers for the interests of some people over the interests of other people. As for a coherent vision, by now it should be obvious to all adults that the lower left cannot deliver on its dream of a world in which no one dominates another; it can only advantage its preferred groups in the struggle for dominance.

In the long run, even the lower left's success will count against it. As the country moves farther away from its European past, the lower left's victimology based on straight-white-male-Christian oppression will seem less and less relevant to daily life. So much of the old world will have passed away that the lower left will have no one left to blame. At the same time, the lower left's anarchical values will thin its own ranks. We have only to look at Europe to see that sooner or later nature will have its say, and those who do not listen shall not thrive. Just as planned economies produce idleness and poverty, family planning and alternative lifestyles produce sterility and extinction.[8] The family-friendly will inherit the earth and stamp it with their own old-fashioned values, and regimes that blind themselves to differences of religion, language, and culture will be gradually restaffed by newcomers who think differently about such things.

The weakness in the lower left raises the possibility that the West might be moving beyond the Age of Anarchy into a new age such as the West has not seen since the triumph of Christianity, an age in which inequalities of wealth and power are unquestioned and the common interest in security and prosperity forces a compromise conclusion to the culture war between the upper right and the lower left. Once the few remaining bones of cultural contention are claimed by one side or the other, the political struggle between good and evil would give way to a new governing consensus based on capitalist assumptions tying the individual interests of the upper left to the corporate interests of the lower right, both governmental and commercial. The regime's principal challenge would be to keep enough individuals satisfied materially to avoid unrest and maintain stability. In effect, what we would see is a collapse of the multipolar politics explained in this book and a return to more bipolar or even unipolar politics, in which matters of governance appear as simple trade-offs between the interests of individuals and the good of the group. The political spectrum would then stretch not simply left and right, but also up and down—from the upper left to the lower right, as it does naturally in all pre-Christian civilizations.

In that case, the conflict between conservatives and liberals would give way in time to competition between an in-group defending its hold on power and an out-group using populist appeals to leverage its bid to take the in-group's place. Between the two, there would be little difference, far less difference than between Republicans and Democrats today, no more perhaps than between Byzantium's Blues and Greens or between Rome's patricians and plebeians in the waning years of the Republic, when wealthy rivals demagogued their way into and out of power, with little difference in the changes of regime. This has already happened in many European countries, where politics has long since ceased to be about cultural issues and is now all about whether government will favor business or people. The American settlement of the remaining cultural issues would no doubt differ from the European settlement, on account of the persistent strength of market-driven American Christianity. But the source of wealth and therefore of power in Europe and America is the same, and so the same interests would drive the political competition.

Many on the Left would say we are there already, and some would say we have been there a long time. Marxism itself was an early reaction against the brave new capitalist world rising out of the Industrial Revolution. But whereas Marx imagined capitalism as a late stage of development, destined to provoke a proletarian revolt that would usher in communism as the final stage, the foregoing suggests that the proletarian revolt has finally failed and that capitalism is returning Western civilization to its natural unipolar, archokratic, pyramidal structure, without the complication of a single unified Christian Church counterbalancing the state.

THE DEMOCRATIC DILEMMA

There is another course that things could take, one based on an estimation of greater persistent strength in the lower left's progressive image-making industry. But to chart that course, the Democratic Party would have to decide which ideal of democracy it represents.

For many years, the Left has based its claim to power on *populist democracy*—an offer of government by the common folk for the benefit of the common folk. That offer has appealed to many people across our Compass, particularly in times when the plutocratic lower right could be portrayed as running things for the benefit of only the rich and oppressing not only the poor, but also individuals and even whole communities. The appeal of populist democracy was the basis of several successful tri-corner coalitions in American history—the patriots of the Revolution, the Democratic-Republicans of the early Republic, the populist Democrats of the Gilded Age, and the New Deal Democrats of the twentieth century.

In the latter half of the twentieth century, however, that last tri-corner Democratic coalition began to suffer under the growing radicalism of the lower left, which has always preferred *progressive democracy* to democracy's populist form. Progressive democracy is an offer of government unrestrained by constitutional tradition, based on a claim of absolute sovereignty for a theoretical construct called "the People." If sovereignty rests solely with the People, then government can be and do whatever the People want. No God, no church, no traditional aristocracy, no customary law, no written constitution can stand in the People's way. If written words cannot be changed, they can instead be reinterpreted, as long as the People agree to go along. Whatever limits real people in the past put on themselves, the People of the present may throw off at will. Everything is subject to change. Progressive democracy makes it possible.

The obvious links between progressive democracy and populist democracy are the assumed identification of the People with the common folk, the general anti-establishment stance, the need for change to reign in the rich and raise up the rest, and the broader power base that the two together can amass.

In their essentials, however, the two differ greatly. The common folk may decide that change is not in their interest and fight to hold on to their accustomed ways, while the People may decide that their progressive interests are better served by the anti-traditional "creative destruction" of democratic capitalism. The common folk might themselves decide they are better off under democratic capitalism, but the disparities of wealth and power created by unrestrained capitalism are an inherent threat to populist democracy. The richer the rich are, the poorer in power the common folk will be. By contrast, capitalism presents no inherent threat to progressive democracy. It does, however, help decide who the People are. Change-hungry progressives expecting to profit greatly under capitalism have therefore less reason to fear capitalism than populist democracy. Capitalism, by enriching them, will give them more power to make the changes they desire; populist democracy could very well threaten that power, either by limiting their financial gain or by voting against their preferred changes. This is the populist threat that progressive elites have long feared.

For decades, Democrats have straddled these two democracies. They have sought to advantage common folk through a variety of measures: tax policies that weigh more heavily on corporations and large estates; regulation of labor relations, occupational safety, consumer product safety, and the environment; tort laws favoring product liability and corporate accountability; welfare for the poor and entitlements like Social Security and subsidized health care for the middle class; trade policy protecting American jobs and communities; and, in the past, tight limits on immigration to save American workers from the ebbless flood of desperately cheap labor and to protect their common European culture from alien challenges.

At the same time, however, Democrats have sought many fundamental changes in the way Americans live their lives, working to secure gay rights, abortion rights, women's rights, affirmative action, gun control, protection of pornography and profanity as free speech, a strict separation of church and state banning prayer and scripture reading in public schools, the use of public education as a replacement for the family and a means of eliminating traditional culture (through sex education, Marxist historical interpretation, affective learning, and the teaching of evolution), the legalization of vices such as gambling, sodomy, public nudity, prostitution, and drug use, and policies to supplant the country's dominant Christian European culture through multicultural immigration and indoctrination.

Notice, though, that there are no necessary connections between the former populist objectives and the latter progressive objectives, no real need to tie abortion rights to trade protection, no necessity for Americans who care about gay rights to also care about Social Security. Democrats only lump the two together because they are still attempting a tri-corner strategy against the power of the lower right. But a strategy placing equal weight on populist objectives to appeal to average Americans and progressive objectives to please the party elites in the lower left is, in this day and age, a sure loser. The party's progressivism turns off voters in the upper right and populist center, while its populism turns off voters in the upper left and lower right.

To manage much more appeal, Democrats must decide which kind of democracy their party represents. This is the identity crisis that has Democrats wondering about their core values. Are they the party of the common man or the progressive elite? Posing as both is no longer possible: The common man isn't buying it. But to try anything else, Democrats will have to give up their self-flattering fantasy of solidarity with all underdogs and admit among themselves that the masses must be ruled.

In recent decades, the trend among Democrats has been toward sacrificing the populist to the progressive. Democrats have switched sides completely on immigration and now angle to replace the working-class whites of their traditional base with working-class Latinos. They have also toned down their insistence on trade protection and progressive taxation, to join Republicans in enacting major pro-business reforms. This has been denounced as selling out by paleo-progressives like Robert Reich at *The American Prospect*, but the trend has been welcomed and encouraged by a new generation of lower-left leaders like Simon Rosenberg, president of the New Democrat Network and founder of the New Politics Institute, one of several new progressive think tanks in search of core values. "Right now it should be clear to progressives that what once worked so well for us no longer does," says Rosenberg. "We need new strategies, new technologies, new techniques and new capacities to meet the challenges of these important times."[9]

New Democrats have a long way to go to first define and then defend a new progressive vision of American democracy, but the challenge would seem far less daunting than resurrecting a realistic tri-corner strategy against the lower right. A broad-based anti-power appeal might work now and then, when imperial Republicans have so disgraced themselves through arrogance and stupidity that a populist tide rises against them.

But a Democratic Party waiting only for such opportunities could never be more than a weak second string. On the other hand, a party anchored in the lower left on progressive social values but fully embracing free-market economics, like the "classical liberals" of the nineteenth century, could reasonably hope to win enough support in the lower right and upper left to remain consistently competitive if not dominant. It all depends on whether there are really enough progressives in the country to pull it off, once they have given up on their more populist appeals.

RED AMERICA

The reader should not mistake the foregoing distinction of populist democracy and progressive democracy for what we sometimes call "social democracy" and "liberal democracy." The former denote two distinct appeals of "democracy" in the minds of men, whereas the latter characterize different aspects of democratic regimes. Commonly understood, social democracies allot a wide role for government in the lives of the people, while liberal democracies allow a wide range of personal freedom. The two are not exclusive: Swedish democracy, for example, can be described as both social and liberal. It is quite another matter, however, whether the Swedish electorate is inspired by the appeal of populist rule or progressive reform. Neither appeal necessarily results in regimes we might call social or liberal. Populist democracy in early nineteenth-century America favored very limited government, whereas progressive democracy in twentieth-century America became increasingly illiberal of traditional freedoms.

These distinctions are worth keeping in mind when Western leaders talk about creating liberal democracies around the world. What they really mean are progressive democracies—regimes without secure rulers, stable constitutions, religious foundations, independent economies, or anything else to safeguard the countries' independence from outside influence. They most certainly do not mean populist democracies when the common folk might freely elect leaders not to Western liking and prefer policies contrary to Western interests. In Eastern Europe, this has meant opposing democracies deemed too religious and traditional, for fear that Christian monarchies and republics might rise again where they once stood. It has meant funding activists pushing progressive agendas such as feminism, secularism, libertinism, and multiculturalism. It has meant vilifying persons and parties that put local interests ahead of NATO's and Wall Street's and publicly endorsing politicians who promise to give the West what it wants.

That both Republican and Democratic administrations pursue progressive democracy abroad with equal enthusiasm should give American conservatives cause to think hard about where the Republican Party is taking them. The GOP's monied interests have always claimed the driver's seat, and until recently the party's values voters could only nag and sulk alongside. The twists and turns of recent events have thrown the two closer together, but they have also uncovered a conflict of visions beneath the Big Tent, between humble patriots and martyrs holding on to permanent things on one hand, and bottom-line bankers and businessmen pursuing profit and power on the other. The latter are prone to regard permanent things with impatience, if not outright hostility. They keep the hostility discreetly covered, but it bares itself at times in the triumphalist propaganda of democratic capitalism, as in these words of Michael Ledeen, former Reagan official and fellow of the American Enterprise Institute:

Creative destruction is our middle name, both within our own society and abroad. We tear down the old order every day, from business to science, literature, art, architecture, and cinema to politics and the law. Our enemies have always hated this whirlwind of energy and creativity, which menaces their traditions (whatever they may be) and shames them for their inability to keep pace. Seeing America undo traditional societies, they fear us, for they do not wish to be undone.... They must attack us in order to survive, just as we must destroy them to advance our historic mission.[10]

If such sentiments seem out of place on the Right, in the "conservative" camp, it must be remembered that the lower right has long been the home of modernizing reform supporting present power, from the enlightened despots of post-Reformation Europe to the revolutionary aristocrats behind Britain's Whig oligarchy and America's early federal republic. In desperate times, as in the early twentieth century when the forces of tradition appeared too weak to beat back Bolshevism's more destructive assaults on the existing order, the lower right has even embraced revolutionary fascism as a lesser evil, even though revolutionary fascism rarely originates within the lower-right establishment and only occupies the lower right after seizing power. This observation presumes a distinction between the more traditional authoritarian regimes of Spain's Franco and Chile's Pinochet, which are native to the lower right, and the more revolutionary—and more truly fascist—authoritarian regimes of Italy's Mussolini and Germany's Hitler, which originated further left in the populist center, in opposition to the Bolshevik lower left. In support of that distinction, let us note that while Franco and Pinochet saw themselves as preserving their nations' traditional culture, Mussolini and Hitler attempted to supplant their nations' traditional culture with an invented ideology informed by fascist theory.

Comparisons to the early, self-styled neoconservatives are impossible to avoid, given the many accusations of fascism hurled against them from other corners. Like the early fascists of Italy and Germany, the early neoconservatives did not originate in the lower right but only migrated to it as a convenient and agreeable source of power. But unlike the fascists of Italy and Germany, the early neoconservatives did not originate in the populist center but in the communitarian deep, with roots extending even further left to the exiled Trotskyites. Ethnically and intellectually, they are more alien in America than the Italian and German fascists were in their own countries. Compared to others on the right, the neoconservatives are more progressive than conservative in their cultural sympathies and more Bolshevik than fascist in their approach to power. This alienation might have made their play for power more difficult, but their own careful scheming, the peculiar psychology of American conservatives, and momentous world events have eased them into power inconspicuously, so that the average "Red" American who votes Republican, watches Fox News, and buys Ann Coulter's books cannot even pick them out. The obvious disharmony between the genuine conservatism of ancient ideals, whether Anglo-American or orthodox Christian, and the ruthlessly new ideology of democratic capitalism à la Ledeen is lost upon the average Red American, who knows only that democracy and capitalism are good and that all who say otherwise are evil.

It remains to be seen how far capitalism will carry us before social conservatives awake to its dangers. When free men are allowed to amass great fortunes from global rackets in gambling, pornography, prostitution, narcotics, weaponry, and usury, the permanent things can only expect short shrift. Ultimately, such unrestrained capitalism is on the side of our enslavers. In a thoroughly capitalist world, men will buy and sell each other. Only a power independent of the free market can save us from the slave market, and only two institutions have shown themselves capable of successfully wielding such power: the essentially kratic organizations of nondemocratic governments that jealously guard against capitalist accumulations of wealth outside government control, and the essentially archic but akratic organization of a unified Christian Church whose material wealth and popular power are committed to nonmarket purposes. Democracy alone is no match for the market, for democracy is itself a market, selling power to the highest bidder.

Notes

CHAPTER 1

1. The following review of Left/Right thinking makes use of David Boaz's *Libertarianism: A Primer* (New York: Free Press, 1997) and Andrew Heywood's *Political Ideologies: An Introduction,* 2nd ed. (New York: Palgrave, 1998).

2. See www.politicalcompass.org, accessed November 5, 2005. The Political Compass appeared earlier on the One World Action Web site at http://64/224/ 165/166/politicalcompass/index.html, accessed July 2, 2001. The One World Action Web site stated that the originators of the compass were "indebted to people like Wilhelm Reich and Theodor Adorno for their ground-breaking work in this field."

3. Political theorists like Johannes Althusius (1557–1638), James Harrington (1611–1677), Henry St. John (Viscount Bolingbroke, 1678–1751), and Baron de Montesquieu (1689–1755) devised various schemes to inhibit the concentration of power in the hands of the already powerful. Their schemes drew more or less on traditional notions of rights, obligations, and divided sovereignty, supplemented with classical and sometimes biblical examples of just government and virtuous citizenship. Bolingbroke was especially popular in the American colonies. John Adams claimed to have read his complete works five times.

4. Later radicals—the martyred Algernon Sidney, polemicists John Trenchard and Thomas Gordon, and the rabble-rousing rake John Wilkes, champion of the American cause in the reign of George III—were generally hostile to clerical authority, "established churches," and the absolute sovereignty of kings or parliaments. They stressed expansion of the franchise, abandonment of feudal rank, abolition of arbitrary power, respect for private property, and wide latitude for personal freedom of conscience and expression. Like Locke, they were very popular in the colonies before the American Revolution. Half of the private libraries in America are believed to have had a copy of *Cato's Letters* by Trenchard and Gordon. Wilkes gave his name to Wilkes-Barre, Pennsylvania; Wilkesboro, North Carolina; and

John Wilkes Boothe. Sidney had Hampden-Sidney College named after him, and in 1825 the governing board of the University of Virginia declared two works to be "generally approved by our fellow citizens" for "general principles of liberty and the rights of man": John Locke's *Second Treatise of Government* and Sidney's *Discourses Concerning Government.*

5. Rousseau saw himself as a latter-day Lycurgus and offered his assistance in lawgiving to Poland and Corsica. Jeremy Bentham aspired to the same honor in England a generation later, writing to President James Madison with an offer to draft a uniform legal code for the United States. Bentham cared nothing for natural rights ("nonsense on stilts") and instead put his faith in simple majoritarian democracy, in effect replacing Rousseau's romantic, intuitive, and very French "general will" with a rationalized, quantified, and very English utilitarian calculus. The great advantage of democracy to progressives is that it frees their hands, making the people the sole source of authority and leaving no one—no pope, no priest, no prince, no patriarch—to tell the people they are wrong.

6. Under feudalism, political sovereignty was understood more as a respon- sibility to enforce the law, not as the right to make it. After the Reformation, the French Catholic Jean Bodin (1530–1596) redefined sovereignty to mean the supreme right to make law, not merely enforce it. The sovereign stood above the law and was therefore not bound by it. Sir Robert Filmer (1588–1653) assigned this absolute sovereignty to the king on account of the king's patriarchal right as father of his country. Jacques-Benigne Bossuet (1627–1704) capped this devel- opment with the "Divine Right of Kings," according to which the king was not obliged to share power with anyone. For Bossuet, the king personified the state. "*Tout l'État est en la personne du prince,*" he wrote, or as the Sun King would say, "*L'État c'est moi.*"

It is thus only in the modern age that Europe's first truly absolute despots appear. At its height, this new absolutism took on the overly ordered aspect of oriental despotism. In 1798, the poet Novalis wrote that "no other state has ever been administered so much like a factory as Prussia since the death of Frederick William." Enlightenment intellectuals were at first enthusiastic fans of absolutism, looking to "enlightened despots" like Frederick of Prussia and Catherine of Russia to rationalize the lives of ignorant, backward, superstitious Europeans.

7. At the Constitutional Convention in 1787, Hamilton declared the British government the best in the world. He advocated life terms for the president and senators, an absolute veto power for the president, and state governors appointed by the central government. In *Federalist* No. 17, he likened the states under the Articles of Confederation to the "feudal anarchy" of medieval Europe and recommended a "more rational and more energetic system of civic polity."

8. As Harvard historian Bernard Bailyn wrote in his Pulitzer Prize winning *The Ideological Origins of the American Revolution:* "To conceive of legislative as- semblies as mirrors of society and their voices as mechanically exact expressions of the people; to assume, and act upon the assumption, that human rights ex- ist above the law and stand as the measure of the law's validity; to understand constitutions to be ideal designs of government, and fixed, limiting definitions

of its permissible sphere of action; and to consider the possibility that absolute sovereignty in government need not be the monopoly of a single all-engrossing agency but (*imperium in imperio*) the shared possession of several agencies each limited by the boundaries of the others but all-powerful within its own—to think in these ways, as Americans were doing before Independence, was to reconceive the fundamentals of government and of society's relation to government." See Bernard Bailyn, *The Ideological Origins of the American Revolution* (Cambridge, MA: Harvard University Press, 1967), p. 230.

CHAPTER 3

1. Michael Lind, *Up from Conservatism: Why the Right Is Wrong for America* (New York: Simon & Schuster, 1996), p. 65.

2. Ibid., p. 67.

3. Daniel P. Moynihan, *Miles to Go: A Personal History of Social Policy* (Cambridge, MA: Harvard University Press, 1996), pp. 74–76.

4. Christopher Hitchens, *No One Left to Lie to: The Values of the Worst Family* (New York: Verso, 2001), p. 141.

5. John B. Judis and Ruy Teixeira, "The Coming Democratic Dominance," *The New Republic*, August 5, 2002.

6. E.J. Dionne, Jr., *Why Americans Hate Politics* (New York: Simon & Schuster, 1991), pp. 15, 17, 24.

7. Progress Policy Institute, "Fact Sheet: About The Third Way," June 1, 1998.

8. Ted Halstead and Michael Lind, *The Radical Center: The Future of American Politics* (New York: Doubleday, 2001), p. 15.

9. Ibid., p. 14.

10. Ibid., pp. 16, 19–20, 25.

11. Ibid., pp. 23, 64.

12. Ibid., p. 25.

13. Ibid., pp. 150, 154, 155.

14. Ibid., p. 170.

15. Ibid., p. 122.

16. Ibid., p. 127.

17. Ibid., pp. 158, 207, 225.

18. Robert D. Putnam, *Bowling Alone: The Collapse and Revival of American Community* (New York: Simon & Schuster, 2000), p. 367.

19. Dana Milbank, "Needed: Catchword for Bush Ideology; 'Communitarian' Finds Favor," *The Washington Post*, February 1, 2001.

20. Amitai Etzioni, *An Immodest Agenda: Rebuilding America Before the 21st Century* (New York: McGraw-Hill Book Co., 1983), p. 25.

21. Ibid., p. 108; Amitai Etzioni, *The Spirit of Community: Rights, Responsibilities, and the Communitarian Agenda* (New York: Crown Publishers, 1993), pp. 57–61.

22. Ibid., pp. 2, 13.

23. Amitai Etzioni, *Next: The Road to the Good Society* (New York: Basic Books, 2001), p. 1.
24. Ibid., p. 4.
25. Ibid., pp. 13, 61.
26. Ibid., pp. 36–37; Etzioni, *The Spirit of Community*, p. 113; Etzioni, *Next*, p. 42.
27. Etzioni, *The Spirit of Community*, pp. 114, 217.
28. Ibid., p. 217; Etzioni, *Next*, pp. 38, 98.

CHAPTER 4

1. David P. Barash, *The L Word: An Unapologetic, Thoroughly Biased, Long-Overdue Explication and Celebration of Liberalism* (New York: William Morrow and Company, 1992).
2. See Paul Edward Gottfried, *After Liberalism: Mass Democracy in the Managerial State* (Princeton, NJ: Princeton University Press, 1999), pp. 13–14. Gottfried cites as his source Arthur A. Ekirch Jr. in *Ideologies and Utopias: The Impact of the New Deal on American Thought* (Chicago: Quadrangle Books, 1969).
3. Cited by Barash, *The L Word*, p. 18. From Solomon Goldman, ed., *The Works of Justice Brandeis* (New York: H. Schuman, 1953).
4. Hillary Rodham Clinton, *It Takes a Village, And Other Lessons Children Teach Us* (New York: Simon & Schuster, 1996), pp. 29, 128.
5. Ibid., p. 14.
6. Barash, *The L Word*, p. 110.
7. Cited by Barash, *The L Word*, p. 96. From Condorcet's *Outline of an Historical View of the Progress of the Human Mind* (Baltimore: G. Fryer, 1802).
8. Barash, *The L Word*, pp. 100–101.
9. Ibid., p. 93.
10. Ibid., p. 101. Ellipsis in the original. See also Theodor W. Adorno, Else Frenkel-Brunswik, Daniel J. Levinson, and R. Nevitt Sanford, *The Authoritarian Personality* (New York: Harper & Brothers, 1950).
11. Barash, *The L Word*, pp. 149, 153.
12. Clinton, *It Takes a Village*, pp. 39, 158, 210.
13. Barash, *The L Word*, pp. 152–153.
14. Robert B. Reich, *Locked in the Cabinet* (New York: Alfred A. Knopf, 1997), p. 13.
15. Paul Wellstone, *The Conscience of a Liberal: Reclaiming the Compassionate Agenda* (New York: Random House, 2001), p. 148.
16. Ibid., p. 149.
17. Cited by Wellstone, *The Conscience of a Liberal*, pp. 142–143; Barash, *The L Word*, p. 95; Wellstone, p. 155.
18. Benjamin R. Barber, *The Truth of Power: Intellectual Affairs in the Clinton White House* (New York: W.W. Norton & Co., 2001), p. 30.
19. Ibid., p. 142.
20. Ibid., p. 156.

21. Ibid., p. 293.

22. Ibid., p. 46.

23. Ibid., p. 174.

24. Ibid., p. 139.

25. Ibid., p. 232.

26. Ibid., pp. 64, 76.

27. Amy Otchet, "Michael Walzer: A User's Guide to Democracy," *UN-ESCO Courier*, January 2000, http://www.unesco.org/courier/2000_01/uk/dires/txt1.htm, accessed March 11, 2002.

28. Max Horkheimer and S.H. Flowerman, in Theodor W. Adorno et al., *The Authoritarian Personality*, p. vii.

29. Terry McAuliffe, chairman of the Democratic National Committee, at the April 2001 Kennedy-King Dinner in Washington, DC.

30. Cited by Michael Lerner, *The Politics of Meaning: Restoring Hope and Possibility in an Age of Cynicism* (Reading, MA: Addison-Wesley Publishing Co., 1996), p. 312.

31. Ibid., p. 3.

32. Ibid., pp. 55, 56, 226, 239–240.

33. Ibid., p. 226.

34. Ibid., p. 233.

CHAPTER 5

1. "I Am Not for World Empire," *The American Conservative*, December 2, 2002, 8–18.

2. Jim Hightower, "Meet Jim," http://www.jimhightower.com/jim/, accessed February 2, 2002.

3. Ruth Conniff, "Barney Frank," *The Progressive*, November 2000, http://www.progressive.org/rc100.htm, accessed May 7, 2001.

4. Ibid.

5. "The Root Is Man," *Memoirs of a Revolutionist*, 1958, p. 29, quoted by Christopher Lasch in his introduction to Richard Hofstadter's *The American Political Tradition and the Men Who Made It* (New York: Vintage Books, 1989), p. xvi.

6. William Greider, *Who Will Tell the People: The Betrayal of American Democracy* (New York: Simon & Schuster, 1992), pp. 28–29, 164.

7. Noam Chomsky, *The Common Good* (Tucson, AZ: Odonian Press, 1998), p. 26; Alexander Cockburn and Ken Silverstein, *Washington Babylon* (New York: Verso, 1996), p. ix; Ralph Nader, *Crashing the Party: Taking on the Corporate Government in an Age of Surrender* (New York: St. Martin's Press, 2002), pp. 13–14.

8. Barbara Ehrenreich, "When Government Gets Mean," *The Nation*, October 7, 1996.

9. David Rieff, "The False Dawn of Civil Society," *The Nation*, February 22, 1999.

10. From Nader, *Crashing the Party*, p. 345.

11. The other co-chairs were talk-show host Phil Donahue, black activist Randall Robinson, and actress Susan Sarandon.

12. David Barsamian, "Noam Chomsky," *The Progressive*, April 16, 2001, www.progressive.org/chom999.htm, is February 12, 2002. Chomsky, *The Common Good*, p. 19.

13. Ibid., p. 7, 8.

14. Ibid., pp. 6, 33, 50, 64.

15. Alexander Cockburn, "25 Years After Vietnam: Beyond Left and Right," *CounterPunch*, April 14, 2000.

16. Ibid.

17. *CounterPunch*, http://www.counterpunch.org/aboutus.html, accessed October 24, 2002.

18. Cockburn and Silverstein, *Washington Babylon*, p. viii.

19. Cockburn, "25 Years After Vietnam."

20. Ibid.

21. Michael Albert, "Anarchism?!" *Znet*, undated, http://www.zmag.org/anarchism.htm, accessed November 11, 2001.

22. Cited by Michael Albert, "Anarchism = Zerzan?" *Znet*, http://www.zmag.org/zerzan.htm, accessed November 14, 2001.

23. Quoted anonymously by Michael Albert, "Albert Replies to Critics of His Anarchism Essay," *Znet*, undated, http://www.zmag.org/anardebate.htm, accessed November 14, 2001.

24. Ibid.

25. Ibid.

26. "Consensus Decision Making," S30 Mobilization for Global Justice, undated, http://www.globalizethis.org/s30/feature.cfm/ID=10, accessed July 13, 2002.

CHAPTER 6

1. F.A. Hayek, *The Road to Serfdom* (Chicago: University of Chicago Press, 1944), Fiftieth Anniversary Edition, 1994, p. 41; Milton Friedman, introduction to preceding, p. xi; David Boaz, *Libertarianism: A Primer* (New York: The Free Press, 1997), p. 106; Virginia Postrel, *The Future and Its Enemies: The Growing Conflict Over Creativity, Enterprise, and Progress* (New York: The Free Press, 1998), p. 142.

2. Boaz, *Libertarianism*, p. 95.

3. Hayek, *The Road to Serfdom*, p. 66.

4. Author's question to Young at the Cato Institute in 2000.

5. "Homosexuals: A Victory for Rationality," *The Economist*, May 25, 1996; *Congressional Record*, Wednesday, June 26, 1996, p. E1174; Linda Greenhouse, "Speaking for the Majority," *The New York Times*, May 26, 1996. The Supreme Court case was *Romer v. Evans*.

6. Gay champion Barney Frank was so pleased that he entered Bolick's words into the *Congressional Record* for Wednesday, June 26, 1996, p. E1174.

7. Ibid., pp. 14–15.

8. Hayek, *The Road to Serfdom*, p. 78.

9. Ibid., p. 257, emphasis in the original.

10. "National Platform of the Libertarian Party," Libertarian Party, http://www.lp.org/issues/platform/, accessed March 6, 2002.

11. "National Platform of the Libertarian Party," Libertarian Party, http://www.lp.org/issues/platform/consmili.html, accessed March 6, 2002.

12. "National Platform of the Libertarian Party," Libertarian Party, http://www.lp.org/issues/platform/famichil.html, accessed March 6, 2002.

13. "National Platform of the Libertarian Party," Libertarian Party, http://www.lp.org/issues/platform/victcrim.html, accessed March 6, 2002; "National Platform of the Libertarian Party," Libertarian Party, http://www.lp.org/issues/platform/famichil.html, accessed March 6, 2002.

14. 1. Hayek, *The Road to Serfdom*, p. 21.

15. Boaz, *Libertarianism*, pp. 5, 26.

16. Postrel, *The Future and Its Enemies*, pp. 217–218.

17. Ibid., p. xiv.

18. Ibid., pp. 112, 116.

19. Ibid., p. 30.

20. Ibid., pp. 32, 33.

21. Boaz, *Libertarianism*, pp. 86, 231.

22. Hayek, *The Road to Serfdom*, p. 65; Boaz, *Libertarianism*, p. 64; "National Platform of the Libertarian Party," Libertarian Party, http://www.lp.org/issues/platform/womenrigh.html, accessed March 6, 2002.

23. Cited by Llewelyn H. Rockwell Jr., "The Case of Paleo-Libertarianism," *Liberty*, January 1990; Jock Friedly, "Cato Institute Finds Hard-Core Supporters in Porn Filmmaker," *The Hill*, July 8, 1998.

24. "About the Author," *Atlas Shrugged* (New York: Plume, 2005).

25. See Chris Matthew Sciabarra, "Understanding the Global Crisis: Reclaiming Rand's Radical Legacy," *The Free Radical*, May/June 2003, and Barry Loberfeld, "The (Tangled) Roots of Objectivist Foreign Policy," LewRockwell.com, Accessed August 23, 2005.

26. Justin Raimondo, "Patriotic Gore," *The American Conservative*, March 1, 2004.

27. Gore Vidal, "Notes on Our Patriarchal State," *The Nation*, September 3, 1990.

28. Gore Vidal, *Rocking the Boat: A Political, Literary, and Theatrical Commentary* (Boston: Little, Brown & Co., 1962), p. 50.

CHAPTER 7

1. Llewelyn H. Rockwell Jr., "The Case for Paleo-Libertarianism," *Liberty*, January 1990.

2. Brian Doherty, "An Interview with Llewellyn H. Rockwell, Jr.," *SpinTech*, May 12, 1999.

3. Murray Rothbard, "A Strategy for the Right," Speech to the John Randolph Club, Chantilly, VA, 1992.

4. Rose Wilder Lane, "Autobiographical Sketch of Rose Wilder Lane," Library of Congress, undated, http://lcweb2.loc.gov/wpa/15100107.html, accessed August 6, 2002.

5. Hans-Hermann Hoppe, "Secession, the State, and the Immigration Problem," LewRockwell.com, May 16, 2001, http://www.lewrockwell.com/orig/hermann-hoppe3.html, accessed May 18, 2001.

6. Dick Armey Reading Room, "Armey's Axioms," http://armey.house.gov/axioms.htm, accessed December 4, 2002.

7. Rockwell, "The Case for Paleo-Libertarianism."

8. Rhys Southan, "Guerrilla Unschooling" (an interview with Grace Llewellyn, author of *The Teenage Liberation Handbook*), *Reason*, October 2001, 17.

9. "35 Heroes of Freedom," *Reason*, December 2003, 65–69.

10. For an insightful contrast between Havel and Klaus, see "Rival Visions," *Journal of Democracy*, 7.1, 1996, 12–23. Accessed October 25, 2002, at http://www.cla.wayne.edu/POLISCI/krause/Easteurope/sources/havel.htm.

11. M. Stanton Evans, *The Theme Is Freedom: Religion, Politics, and the American Tradition* (Washington, DC: Regnery Publishing, 1994), p. 38.

12. Ibid., pp. 315, 318.

13. Ibid., p. 111. Emphasis in the original.

14. Ibid., p. 319.

15. Ibid., p. 323.

16. Ibid., p. 321. Emphasis in the original.

17. Ibid., p. 313. Emphasis in the original.

18. Ibid., p. 343.

19. Harry Browne, *Why Government Doesn't Work* (New York: St. Martin's Press, 1995), p. 1.

20. Ibid., pp. 2–3.

21. Ibid., pp. 10, 12, 28.

22. Ibid., pp. 140, 142–143.

23. Ibid., pp. 39, 47.

24. Hans-Hermann Hoppe, *Democracy: The God That Failed* (New Brunswick, NJ: Transaction Publishers, 2001), pp. xx, 16.

25. Ibid., p. xx.

26. Ibid., p. xxi.

CHAPTER 8

1. Joseph Sobran, "The Timorous Intellectuals," *Chronicles*, May 2002, 15.

2. See Paul Gottfried, *The Conservative Movement*, Revised Edition (New York: Twayne Publishers, 1993), pp. 74–75.

3. David Frum, *Dead Right* (New York: Basic Books, 1994), p. 126.

4. George Nash, *The Conservative Intellectual Movement in America: Since 1945* (Wilmington, DE: Intercollegiate Studies Institute, 1996), p. 63.

5. Ibid.

6. Ibid., pp. 62, 64.

7. Ibid., p. 62.

8. Ibid., p. 68.

9. See John Zmirak, *Whilhelm Ropke: Swiss Localist, Global Economist* (Wilmington, DE: ISI Books, 2001).

10. See Patrick Allitt, *Catholic Intellectuals and Conservative Politics in America, 1950–1985* (Ithaca, NY: Cornell University Press, 1993), pp. 75–77.

11. See Thomas Fleming, "Abusing Your Illusions," *Chronicles*, January 2002, 10–12, 72; Chilton Williamson Jr., "Promises to Keep," in *The Paleoconservatives: New Voices of the Old Right*, Joseph Scotchie, ed. (New Brunswick, NJ: Transaction Publishers, 1999), p. 100.

12. Patrick J. Buchanan, *The Death of the West: How Dying Populations and Immigrant Invasions Imperil Our Country and Civilization* (New York: St. Martin's Press, 2002), p. 229; Gottfried, *The Conservative Movement*, pp. 112–113.

13. See Richard Hofstadter, *The Age of Reform* and *The American Political Tradition and the Men Who Made It* (New York: Alfred Knopf, 1948). Hofstadter writes that many Progressives were old-money men who saw their "status" being eclipsed by the new-money magnates of the Gilded Age and who rose in reaction to represent populist interests so as to regain their status.

14. See Hamilton Fish, *Memoir of an American Patriot* (Washington, DC: Regnery Gateway, 1991).

15. Recent historians have shown that Fish was more right than wrong on that score.

16. The American Cause, "About the Cause," http://www.theamericancause.org/about.htm, accessed June 13, 2001.

17. Howard Phillips, *The Next Four Years: A Vision of Victory* (Franklin, TN: Adroit Press, 1992), p. 16.

18. Ibid., p. 157; Constitution Party National Internet HQ, "Constitution Party 2000 National Platform," http://www.constitutionparty.com/ustp-99pl.html, accessed May 1, 2002.

19. Kevin Phillips, "Why I Am No Longer a Conservative," *The American Conservative*, October 7, 2002.

20. Kevin Phillips, *Wealth and Democracy* (New York: Broadway Books, 2002), p. 420.

21. Buchanan, *The Death of the West*, pp. 1–2, 5.

22. "The Conservative Vision," *Crisis*, June 24, 1955, 295–299, cited in Allitt, *Catholic Intellectuals and Conservative Politics*, p. 145.

23. Thomas Fleming, "Foreword," *Chronicles*, November 2001, 2.

24. Thomas Fleming, "Cultural Revolutions," *Chronicles*, January 2002, 6.

25. Samuel Francis, "Neo-Con Invasion," *The New American*, August 5, 1996.

26. Joseph Sobran, "Anarchism, Reason, and History," Sobran's, January 24, 2002, http://www.sobran.com/columns/020124.shtml, accessed January 24, 2002.

CHAPTER 9

1. Cal Thomas and Ed Dobson, *Blinded By Might: Can the Religious Right Save America?* (Grand Rapids, MI: Zondervan Publishing House, 1999), p. 11.

2. Pat Robertson, "Restore States Rights and Public Morality," Speech delivered to the Yale University Law School, March 25, 1986.

3. Pat Robertson, "A Presidential Bid Launched," September 17, 1986, http://www.patrobertson.com/Statesman/PresidentialBidLaunched.asp, accessed May 23, 2002.

4. On Bryan, see Richard Hofstadter, *The American Political Tradition And the Men Who Made It* (New York: Vintage Books, 1989), pp. 241–264.

5. See Patrick Allitt, *Catholic Intellectuals and Conservative Politics in America: 1950–1985* (Ithaca, NY: Cornell University Press, 1993), pp. 70–82.

6. Richard John Neuhaus, *Doing Well & Doing Good: The Challenge to the Christian Capitalist* (New York: Doubleday, 1992), p. 187.

7. Pat Robertson, "A Presidential Bid Launched," Speech delivered at Constitution Hall, Washington, DC, September 17, 1986, http://www.patrobertson.com/Statesman/PresidentialBidLaunched.asp, accessed May 23, 2002.

8. Marvin Olasky, *Compassionate Conservatism: What It Is, What It Does, And How It Can Transform America* (New York: The Free Press, 2000), pp. 3, 182.

9. Robert H. Bork, *Slouching Towards Gomorrah: Modern Liberalism and American Decline* (New York: HarperCollins, 1996), p. 342.

10. Ibid., p. 6.

11. Ibid., pp. 6, 7.

12. Alan Keyes, "Declaration Foundation Inaugural Address," August 11, 1996, http://www.sandh.com/Keyes/df081196.htm, accessed June 13, 2001.

13. "Religion's Role in Public Life," *Religion & Liberty*, Acton Institute for the Study of Religion & Liberty, September–October 1993.

14. Ralph Reed, *Politically Incorrect: The Emerging Faith Factor in American Politics* (Dallas, TX: Word Publishing, 1994), p. 39.

15. "The End of Democracy? The Judicial Usurpation of Politics," *First Things*, November 1996, 18, at http://www.firstthings.com/ftissues/ft9611/articles/eodmaster.html, accessed May 21, 2002.

16. See Jacob Heilbrunn, "Neocon v. Theocon: The New Fault Line on the Right," *The New Republic*, December 30, 1996, at http://magazines.enews.com/archive/1996/12/123096/heilbrunn123096.html, accessed September 24, 2002.

17. Marvin Olasky, "National Greatness: Looking for Purpose in All the Wrong Places," *World*, November 15, 1997.

18. Quoted by Thomas and Dobson, *Blinded By Might*, p. 248. See also Pat Robertson, "Restore America to Its Jeffersonian Ideals," Speech to the Jefferson Literary and Debating Society at the University of Virginia, March 3, 2000.

19. Press release and membership list of the Constitution Project Initiative on Liberty and Security, published by The Constitution Project of the Public Policy Institute, Georgetown University, November 13, 2001.

20. Brian Mitchell, "Are Conservatives in Trouble After Exodus of Leadership?" *Investor's Business Daily*, December 18, 2001.

CHAPTER 10

1. George Nash, *The Conservative Intellectual Movement in America: Since 1945* (Wilmington, DE: Intercollegiate Studies Institute, 1996), pp. 11–12; John P. East, *The American Conservative Movement: The Philosophical Founders* (Chicago: Regnery Books, 1986), p. 81.

2. On the limits of Buckley's libertarianism, see Patrick Allitt, *Catholic Intellectuals and Conservative Politics in America 1950–1985* (Ithaca, NY: Cornell University Press, 1993), pp. 73–74.

3. East, *The American Conservative Movement*, pp. 105–142.

4. Mark Gerson, *The Neoconservative Vision: From the Cold War to the Culture Wars* (Lanham, MD: Madison Books, 1996), pp. 16–19.

5. "The Adversary Culture and the New Class," in B. Bruce-Briggs, ed., *The New Class?* (New Brunswick, NJ: Transaction Books, 1979), pp. 30–131. Cited by Michael Lind, *Up from Conservatism: Why the Right Is Wrong for America* (New York: Simon & Schuster, 1996), p. 65.

6. Irving Kristol, *Neoconservatism: The Autobiography of an Idea* (New York: Simon & Schuster, 1995), p. 128.

7. Willmoore Kendall, "Who Killed Political Philosophy?" *National Review*, March 12, 1960. Quoted by East, *The American Conservative Movement*, p. 144.

8. Kristol, *Neoconservatism*, p. 7.

9. Ibid.

10. Ibid., p. 8.

11. Ibid.; Leo Strauss, "On the Intention of Rousseau," *Social Research*, XIV, December, 1947, 485. Quoted by East, *The American Conservative Movement*, pp. 148–149.

12. Leo Strauss, *Natural Right and History* (Chicago: University of Chicago Press, 1953), p. 6. Quoted by Nash, *The Conservative Intellectual Movement in America*, p. 45.

13. See Irving Kristol, "Why Religion Is Good for the Jews," *Commentary*, August 1994.

14. Ronald Bailey, "The Voice of Neoconservatism," *Reason*, October 17, 2001.

15. William J. Bennett, *The Book of Virtues: A Treasury of Great Moral Stories* (New York: Simon & Schuster, 1993), p. 741.

16. William J. Bennett, *The De-Valuing of America: The Fight for Our Culture and Our Children* (New York: Summit Books, 1992), pp. 210, 211.

17. Norman Podhoretz, "Neoconservatism: A Eulogy," Speech to the American Enterprise Institute, January 16, 2001.

18. "Up Close and Personal with Rich Lowry," *The Stanford Review*, October 13, 2000; Irving Kristol, "The Coming 'Conservative Century,'" *Wall Street Journal*, February 1, 1993; Kristol, *Neoconservatism*, p. 365. Cf. Theocon Gary Bauer's "pro-life, pro-family, pro-growth" motto. D'Souza's words are from his public remarks at the American Enterprise Institute, October 10, 2002.

19. Michael Novak, *The Spirit of Democratic Capitalism* (New York: Simon & Schuster, 1982), p. 14; Quoted by Gerson, *The Neoconservative Vision*, p. 199.

20. Michael Novak, "The Crisis of the Welfare State," *Crisis*, July/August 1993; Irving Kristol, "The Two Welfare States," *The Wall Street Journal*, October 19, 2000; George W. Bush, *A Charge To Keep* (New York: William Morrow and Company, 1999), p. 229.

21. Ibid., p. 230.

22. Irving Kristol, "The Two Welfare States," *The Wall Street Journal*, October 19, 2000.

23. David Brooks, "A Return to National Greatness: Manifesto for a Lost Creed," *The Weekly Standard*, February 24, 1997.

24. William Kristol and Robert Kagan, "Toward a Neo-Reaganite Foreign Policy," *Foreign Affairs*, July/August, 1996.

25. Max Boot, "The Case for American Empire," *The Weekly Standard*, October 15, 2001.

26. Patrick J. Buchanan, "Whose War?" *The American Conservative*, March 24, 2003.

27. David Frum, "Unpatriotic Conservatives: A War against America," *National Review*, April 7, 2003.

28. John J. Mearsheimer and Stephen M. Walt, "The Israel Lobby and U.S. Foreign Policy," Harvard University John F. Kennedy School of Government, March 2006.

29. Francis Fukuyama, "After Neoconservatism," *The New York Times*, February 19, 2006.

CHAPTER 11

1. Jeff Dufour, "Webb Seeks Return to Democratic Roots," *Alexandria Times*, April 6–13, 2006.

2. Ibid.

3. "Jim Webb Liveblogging Right Now," *Daily Kos*, March 30, 2006, http://www.dailykos.com/story/2006/3/30/173556/216, accessed May 23, 2006.

4. "Born Fighting: Jim Webb for U.S. Senate," *Webb for Senate*, undated, http://www.webbforsenate.com/issues/issues.php#econ, accessed May 23, 2006.

5. Dufour, "Webb Seeks Return to Democratic Roots."

6. Dufour, "Webb Seeks Return to Democratic Roots."

7. Democrats have complained of the success of such conservative think tanks, funded by conservative foundations such as Bradley, Olin, and Scaife, but the lower left has foundations of its own much larger than those of the lower right. John Micklethwait and Adrian Wooldridge write: "The big conservative foundations are minnows compared with liberal behemoths like the Ford, Rockefeller, and MacArthur foundations. Bradley gives out less money in a year than Ford does in a month." *The Right Nation* (New York: Penguin Press, 2004), p. 166.

8. See Phillip Longman, "The Return of Patriarchy," *Foreign Policy*, March/April 2006. A fellow of the New America Foundation, Longman writes: "The 17.4 percent of baby boomer women who had only one child account for a mere 7.8 percent of

children born in the next generation. By contrast, nearly a quarter of the children of baby boomers descend from the mere 11 percent of baby boomer women who had four or more children."

9. New Democrat Network press release, "NDN Launches the New Politics Institute," May 10, 2005.

10. Michael Ledeen, *The War against the Terror Masters* (New York: St. Martin's Press, 2002), pp. 212–213.

Index

About the Author

BRIAN PATRICK MITCHELL is the Washington Bureau Chief of *Investor's Business Daily*. As a veteran political reporter and author, Mitchell has appeared on dozens of television and radio shows, including *Face the Nation, Larry King Live, Today, Crossfire*, and *Nightline*. He also has been a guest speaker at Harvard's Kennedy School of Government, the University of Pennsylvania, the University of Connecticut, and Catholic University of America.